HIPAA Healthy

Useful Tips & Best Practices for Providers

Copyright © 2016 Spiffy Press, a division of Spiffy Solutions Inc. All rights reserved.

No part of this publication may be reproduced, stored in a retrieval system, or transmitted in any form or by any means, electronic, mechanical, photocopying, recording, scanning, or otherwise, except as permitted under Section 107 or 108 of the 1976 United States Copyright Act, without the prior written permission of the publisher. Requests to the publisher for permission should be addressed in writing to Spiffy Press, 3020 I Prosperity Church Road 136, Charlotte, North Carolina 28269 or online at http://www.spiffypresspublishing.com.

ISBN-13: 978-0-692-73826-9
ISBN-10: 0-692-73826-6

Limit of Liability/Disclaimer of Warranty: While the publisher and author have used their best efforts in preparing this book, they make no representation or warranties with respect to the accuracy or completeness of the contents of this book and specifically disclaim any implied warranties of merchantability or fitness for a particular purpose. No warranty may be created or extended by sales representatives or written sales materials. The advice and strategies contained herein may not be suitable for your situation. You should consult with a professional where appropriate. Nether the publisher nor the author shall be liable for any loss of profit or any other commercial damages, including but not limited to special, incidental, consequential, or other damages.

Readers should be aware that Internet Websites offered as citations and/or sources for further information may have changed or disappeared between the time this book was written and when it is read.

Spiffy Press also publishes its books in a variety of electronic formats. Some content that appears in print may not be available in electronic books.

*To Melissa, Tanner and Kara
for always supporting
my crazy ideas.*

Table of Contents

Introduction 1
   What Is HIPAA? 1
   Who Should Read This Book 2
   Technical Knowledge Is Required 2
   What You Will Learn from This Book 3
   Getting The Most Out of This Book 4
   Icons Used in This Book 4
   Meeting the Security Rule standards 5
   A Final Word 5

Understanding Server-Client Architecture 7
   An Introduction to Servers 8
   Building the "Perfect" Server 14
   Purchasing a New Server 16
   An Introduction to BitLocker 17
   Turn on BitLocker in Windows 2012 19
   Summary 22
   Up Next 22

Configure a Domain 23
   What is a Domain? 24
   The Power of Active Directory and Policies 25
   Getting Started with Active Directory 26
   Protecting User Passwords is a Must 33
   How Active Directory Controls Passwords 33
   Summary 35
   Up Next 36

The Internet Affects Your Security 37
   Time Wasters and Malicious Sites 37
   Malicious Sites Are Out to Get You 38
   Who Let the (Malware) in? 39
   The Dangers of Social Engineering 40
   Ways to Protect Yourself Against Internet Threats 42
   Enforcing Automatic Updates Across your Domain 43
   Good Free and Paid Antivirus Programs 45

Clean your Traffic with a Good Web Filter 47
Summary 49
Up Next 49

The Cloud Brings More than Rain 51
Dealing with Cloud Providers 52
Business Associate Agreements 53
Securing Email 54
Long Term Email Archival 54
Enterprise Level Email 56
Stop Spam Dead 57
Encrypted Mail 58
Summary 60
Next Up 60

Protecting Your Network with a Firewall 61
Why You Should Have a Firewall 61
Logging Firewall Events 63
Control Internet Traffic 65
Virtual Private Networks and Remote Access 66
Prevent Personal Devices from Accessing your Network 66
Summary 68
Up Next 68

Protecting Your Wireless Network 69
Do's and Don'ts of Wi-Fi 70
Identifying Devices 71
Consider the Risks 72
Using Separated Protected and Open Wireless Networks ... 74
Built-in vs Dedicated? 75
Firewalls with Wi-Fi Capability 76
Standalone Wi-Fi Access Points 77
Configuring a Wireless Access Point 78
Hiding your Wireless from Snooping Eyes 78
Summary 80
Up Next 80

Managing EPHI On Your Server 81
Keeping Everything Organized 81
Security Management Process §164.308(a)(1) 81
Performing a Risk Assessment 82
Using Partitions to Organize Data 84

Redirect Folders to the Server	89
Create a Folder for Shared Files	94
Summary	95
Up Next	95

User Accounts and File Level Security 97

Users and Groups, Oh My!	97
File and Folder Permissions	100
Sharing Permissions	100
Setting Access Permissions	101
Summary	106
Up Next	106

Backing Up Your Data 107

Types of Backups	108
Choosing Storage for Your Backups	111
Encrypting Your Backups	113
Disaster Recovery Plan	115
Summary	118
Up Next	118

Enforcing Policies on Your Network 119

Handling Policy Violations	120
Enforcing Policies	121
Setting a Password Policy	121
Disabling the Guest Account	122
Other Policies	123
Locking the Screensaver with a Password	124
Automatic Logoff	126
Stop Password Sharing	126
Use Biometric Devices to Avoid Typing Passwords	128
Written Policies and Training	130
Summary	133
Up Next	133

Audit and Monitoring 135

Definition of Logs	135
Logging and Reporting Requirements	136
Collecting Logs	137
Employee Monitoring Tools	139
Event Log Monitors	141
A Combination Approach	143

- Information System Activity Review ... 143
- Security Incident Procedures ... 144
- Summary ... 146
- Up Next ... 146

Physical and Environmental Safeguards ... 147
- Physical Security ... 147
- Chain of Trust ... 150
- USB Flash Drives and Removable Media ... 151
- Workstation Usage Policies and Procedures ... 151
- Encrypting Data ... 152
- Handling Devices and Removable Media ... 152
- Re-Using Media and Devices ... 153
- Continued Training ... 154
- Summary ... 155

Final Summary ... 157

Index ... 161

About the Author

Andy Raphael has a passion for technology and helping small businesses succeed by using technology in their day-to-day business. From starting his career as an IT administrator in education to successfully operating an IT consulting company, he has accumulated a lot of knowledge over his 20 year career. It was here that he was able to develop his methods and fine tune them to help healthcare professionals, and now he has brought his knowledge to you in the form of techniques that people can follow.

I Want to Hear from You!

As the reader of this book, *you* are my most important critic, my audience and my listener. I value your opinion and want to know what I'm doing right, what I could do better, what other areas you might like to see me publish in, and any other bits of information you want to pass on to me.

You can send me an email to let me know what you liked about this book, or what you thought I could have done better. I take the good with the bad. It's how we all become better.

Please understand that I can't help you with technical problems related to the topics of this book. For that I recommend you contact someone who can meet with you in person. Also, due to the high volume of mail I receive, I might not be able to reply to every message. Just know that I appreciate hearing from you!

Email: feedback@spiffypresspublishing.com

Reader Services

Visit my website and register this book at www.spiffypresspublishing.com/register for convenient access to any updates, downloads, or errata that might be available for this book.

Introduction

We live in a digital age where computer networking is necessary to run a successful business. Access to the Internet, data sharing, document imaging, and email are all common practices in the modern office setting. Sensitive data is shared among office staff, but this data must be protected from threats, electronic hackers, or data loss. It's a common misconception that hackers only target big companies. Smaller offices with minimal security and computer defenses are easier to target, and gaining access to patient data through these businesses provides the hacker with a highly marketable product on the black market.

What Is HIPAA?

The Health Insurance Portability and Accountability Act of 1996 (HIPAA) sets forth requirements and standards to help healthcare providers store, maintain and manage patient data. These guidelines protect patient data from eavesdroppers and provide an audit trail to make providers accountable for mishandling sensitive data.

 Link: The official website of the HIPAA Privacy Rule is operated by the US government and is located at http://www.hhs.gov/hipaa/for-professionals/privacy/

Unfortunately, most healthcare providers don't have the necessary technical skills to understand what's required to protect electronically protected health information (EPHI), also known as personally identifiable information (PII) or personal health information (PHI). You may think that small changes to your office's technology don't create a HIPAA violation, but hackers find ways of implementing their attacks even from the smallest security mistake. HIPAA requires healthcare providers to understand the ramifications of leaking data, but how is a provider supposed to know when a change might create a security hole?

Who Should Read This Book

My goal is to help healthcare providers better understand HIPAA, EPHI, digital security, networking topology, and technology which can be used to implement the most secure protection of their data. This book is meant to be used as a set of guidelines for any small healthcare practitioner whether you are office staff or an IT professional in charge of small office networks.

This book isn't an exhaustive guide to all things HIPAA. The book's goal is to help healthcare providers build a networking environment that's safe for patients and office staff alike. It's meant to help providers understand the importance of technology for HIPAA standards. Remember, hackers are looking for any information that they can find and steal and sell on the black market.

 Note: Office staff PII is also useful for the hacker, so any human resources data should also be stored in a secure environment.

The blueprint laid out in this book also isn't an end-all solution. Electronic hackers continue to find innovative ways to bypass security, so the technology industry is always changing the way it protects user information. Technology changes each year, so a savvy small business person knows that the proper way to secure network today might not be the best way tomorrow.

Technical Knowledge Is Required

Let's be honest. I'd love to be able to provide you a simple guide that you can implement without even the slightest bit of technical knowledge. The truth is that it takes many IT professionals years to master these skills and understand the complexity of networks, servers, firewalls, and security. Many of the examples shown throughout this book are not for the faint of heart and are actually quite complex. By no means am I suggesting that you attempt to do all these steps by yourself. **Instead, hiring a qualified IT expert is my number one advice when it comes to building and maintaining a reliable, HIPAA compliant network.**

 Tip: Before hiring an IT expert or Managed Service Provider, use the information from this book to conduct interviews with as many candidates as you can. Too often, even experts in the field are not familiar with HIPAA and its regulations.

You can use the examples that you learn in this book as a foundation of knowledge so that you can conduct educated conversations and discussions with your IT service provider. The contents of this book should give you a basic understanding of the steps needed to be on your way to HIPAA compliance. (Besides HIPAA related material, it's also an excellent way to secure and protect any office network.)

What You Will Learn from This Book

I have structured the content of this book to provide you with the understanding and knowledge on the rule titled "Security Standards for the Protection of Electronic Protected Health Information", found at 45 CFR Part 160 and Part 164, Subparts A and C, commonly known as the Security Rule.

In this book I am going to show you, the reader, real world practical examples and implementations of the Security Rule. After reading this book, you will be able to implement our examples into your own office or private practice.

Also keep in mind that with a little understanding, you can use this blueprint and tweak it in a way that works for your office environment. Think of this blueprint as the starting point, and then use it to structure your own network infrastructure.

This guide will provide you with some basics including:
- **Setting up a domain and Windows server**
- **Working on the Internet and identifying malicious content and downloads**
- **Protecting your network with a firewall**
- **Setting up wireless capabilities in your office**
- **Backing up your data**
- **Enforcing security policies on your network**
- **Logging (auditing) files and Active Directory**

Getting The Most Out of This Book

I'll cover many examples and use vendor-specific applications in some instances, but I don't endorse any specific vendor. Vendors are used just to provide an example, but you can use your own applications and vendors to customize this blueprint.

Note: I am not a legal advisor. I am a technology professional who is providing you with building blocks for a more secure environment. If you have specific questions regarding HIPAA regulations and the law, you should consult a lawyer.

Icons Used in This Book

Throughout this book I will highlight important details with icons to make it easier for you to see things at a glance.

Tips are useful bits of the explanation that emphasize a point. They aren't always the only way to get something done, but they do point out a way to accomplish a task you might have missed.

The Note icon is used to point out an additional explanation of what's been said or why you need to do something I've mentioned.

 When you see the Link icon I want to highlight a website link that contains important or useful information that you may want to read.

Meeting the Security Rule standards

Each Security Rule[1] standard with respect to EPHI (see 45 C.F.R §164.302) must be met in compliance. Small providers that are covered entities have unique situations in the way they operate that provide both opportunities and challenges related to compliance with the Security Rule. In this book I am going to address each Security Rule and give practical examples to aid in understanding the requirements.

Implementation specifics are either *required* or *addressable*. All required implementation must be complied with, regardless of cost, size, technical infrastructure or resources.

A Final Word

The HIPAA website provides resources to learn more about the Security Rule. This book's goal is to emphasize practical understanding of the rules, instead of regurgitating rules and regulations that can be found elsewhere.

Finally, I will use acronyms throughout this book. At the end of the book is a glossary of terms to define these acronyms. I'll try to explain them fully within each chapter, but use the glossary terms if you're not familiar with any methodology or service description.

---

[1] In this book I'm only going to focus on aspects of the security rule as they apply to computers and networks in a small business environment. Larger organizations that need multiple servers, have more than one location, or employ a larger workforce may have requirements exceeding the scope of this book.

1
Understanding Server-Client Architecture

It's very common for a small office to use a workgroup environment. A workgroup is several computers set up to communicate over a network and equally share all responsibilities and storage. Unfortunately, this type of environment is extremely insecure and involves no accountability from users. They aren't HIPAA compliant, so any healthcare office must upgrade to server-client architecture.

Workgroup environments are attractive to small healthcare providers, because they don't take a lot of technical know-how to set up, and they are easy to maintain. They are referred to as peer-to-peer networks. Every computer can communicate with each other and security isn't granular.

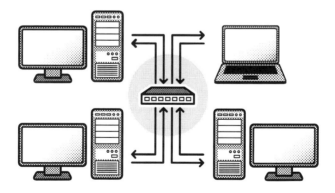

Figure 1. A simple peer-to-peer workgroup is a network of independent computers.

If your office is set up similar to the image above, then you're using a workgroup environment. Another way to identify if you're using this type of environment is to look at your Windows settings.

You can find network properties in the Windows Control Panel in the System and Security settings. For instance, if you're running Windows 7, right click the "Computer" icon in the main menu and select "Properties." Network properties are found in this screen.

Figure 2. The workgroup name can be found in the System screen.

In the example above, the computer is a part of a small home office, so a workgroup is sufficient. However, it's not an office environment working with EPHI. Your home office can work within a workgroup environment, but any network in a healthcare office should be a server-client setup.

An Introduction to Servers

At first, you might think moving to a server environment is too much trouble. It's also more expensive, and it requires more maintenance and technical know-how to configure. However, it offers many benefits and advantages, even beyond HIPAA compliance.

Servers centralize everything about your network including file storage, security, policies, backups and logging. This one central device can be used to control all aspects of the network.

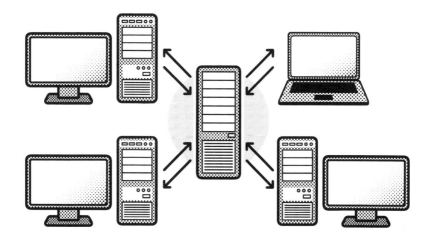

Figure 3. In a Server-Client environment all devices communicate directly with the server.

The server should never be used as a personal computer. In other words, don't buy an expensive machine just to have the front desk use it for productivity. The server is always a "hands off" computer that no one but key personnel have access to. Not only is it bad for security to use it as a workstation, but it also harms performance. For instance, if your front office staff installs several personal programs on the server, they can interfere with legitimate office files and programs.

 Tip: *A server is always a hands-off device that should be placed in a secure location.*

Servers are workhorses, so installing a common desktop in the office is never sufficient. The server is responsible for much more than just word processing and email. The server must be able to handle all aspects of network policies, file management and any application requests. A desktop isn't built for this type of performance requirements. You need powerful and dedicated resources to serve all of your current staff and any future personnel. You can buy a custom built machine or use one of the popular vendors available.

When shopping for a server, you should look for three main component specs: CPU, memory and storage. There are other components that make a good server, but these are the three that you should be concerned with.

CPU

Figure 4. The CPU is the "brains" of the computer.

All activity on the server is sent to the Central Processing Unit (CPU) for execution. In the early 2000s, CPU manufacturers maxed out speed capabilities, so they were forced to create several CPUs within one chip. These CPUs are called "cores." You'll find that servers are packed with several cores. The number of cores you need is dependent on the amount of work that's going to be done on the server.

If your server is only used for file storage, you don't need as many cores as a server that runs several applications for your office. For a small office, 2 to 4 cores are sufficient.

Memory

Figure 5. Random Access Memory holds data as it's sent to the CPU.

Random access memory (RAM) is the fastest storage unit of the computer. RAM holds data as it's sent to the CPU. Because your CPU can't process everything at once, you need RAM. RAM is also used when you open an application and keep it open until you're finished with it. RAM is a major component for performance. If you don't have enough RAM, the server uses the hard drive as a backup. Since a hard drive is not as fast as RAM, this causes performance degradation.

Similar to CPU requirements, the amount of RAM you need will depend on the workload. A good start for a server is about 16GB of RAM, but you could need less or more depending on performance needs. You can always add more RAM as needed, so don't worry if it turns out you ordered a computer with a bit less than you need.

Storage

Figure 6. Servers often use several hard drives to store data.

Of all the resource requirements in a small office, storage is probably the most important to consider. Drives are used for file storage and backups, and they factor into server speed. You also need a drive "system." These systems are called RAID (Redundant Array of Independent Disks). RAID has several levels, but I recommend RAID 5. RAID 5 requires at least three storage disks. Data is spread across all disks, which improves security and speed.

The benefit of RAID 5 is that you get data redundancy (in case a drive fails) and better performance. If one drive fails, the others can take its place[2]. Your users will still be able to work as usual without interruption. Since all drives serve data to the CPU, you also get faster processing speeds. Of course, if a drive fails, you should replace it as soon as possible, but at least you won't lose money due to lost productivity and downtime.

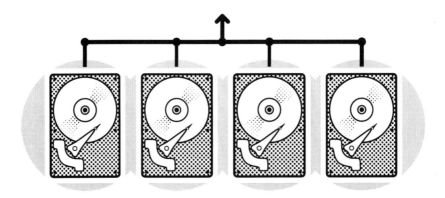

Figure 7. Multiple hard drives in RAID 5 provide redundancy.

In addition to the drive configuration, servers usually offer different options for disks. You might find hard disks labelled as SATA, SAS, Near-Line SAS, or even Solid State. At this point SAS drives are the best option, because they have many benefits over other drives. SAS drives perform better than SATA drives and have proven to be much more reliable than SATA in the long term. Solid state drives for servers are (as of the writing of this book) more expensive, although in a few

---

[2] There are many different types of RAID configurations, but RAID 5 is one of the most popular options for entry level servers.

years their price will likely be extremely competitive to SAS drives, if they don't replace them altogether.

Overall, server resources are far more powerful than a desktop, which is why you see an increase in cost. Some other server advantages include:

- Central data storage – you no longer need to search every workgroup computer for a file that you need.
- Easier ways to back up – backups are controlled and maintained from one server, so you don't have to back up a dozen (or more!) PCs individually.
- Easier security management – control policies and network security from one machine.
- Store data in one location – storing your data in one location is better for maintenance but also for security. Hackers can only access your data from one location, which you will have completely secured.

 Note: When you move to a client-server architecture, you'll need to move data from office computers to the server. No EPHI should ever be stored on individual computers. All folders that store this type of data are redirected to the server through policies, which we will discuss in later chapters.

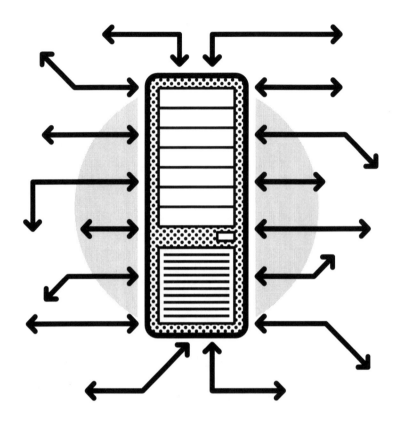

Building the "Perfect" Server

At this point, you're probably thinking "Just tell me the perfect server for me to buy." In reality, the optimal server is one that meets your specific needs and is configured in a way that exceeds your current requirements, so that it will be able to handle additional software and services in the future.

The following table is an example of a server suitable for a small healthcare practitioner's office. In this example, as well as our continued discussion in the remaining chapters of this book, I'm going to focus on a hypothetical business that has 3 to 6 employees.

Sample configuration of a typical server (2016)

Option	Description
Dell PowerEdge T330	Dell's line of servers offer a lot of customizability and their onsite warranty means a technician will come to your place of business to make hardware repairs when needed.
TPM	The Trusted Platform Module is required to encrypt your server's operating system.
4 Core Intel Xeon CPU	Stay away from any CPU that is not Xeon.
16GB memory	This amount is the sweet spot between performance and cost.
RAID 5 with PERC H730	The hardware controller allows the server's hard drive to operate at full speed.
15K RPM SAS hard drives	You will need at least 3 of them to configure as a RAID 5.
Bezel (front)	Dell offers this as optional component, but you will need it later to lock access to the hard drives with a key.
Operating System	Microsoft Windows Server 2012 R2 Standard.
Client Access Licenses	5-pack of Windows Server 2012 Device CALs (make sure to cover all computers that will connect to your server).
Warranty	I highly recommend a minimum of 3 or 5 years, since it will be much cheaper than purchasing an extended warranty in the future.
Total cost	Around $3,500 to $4,000.

Purchasing a New Server

Now that you know the benefits of using a server in your office, you might wonder how and where servers can be purchased. The answer is that you buy a server much like you would a normal desktop, except you can't drive to a local big box store (for example Best Buy or Staples) and pick up a server from what they have in stock.

Typically, servers are ordered directly from a major computer manufacturer by selecting the options and features you require. The manufacturer will then customize the hardware to your specifications and ship it to your business.

Popular Server Manufacturers in the United States

Manufacturer	Website	Phone Number
Dell	http://www.dell.com	1-800-456-3355
HP	http://www.hpe.com	1-855-472-5233
Lenovo	http://www.lenovo.com	1-866-426-0911

An Introduction to BitLocker

BitLocker was introduced with Windows Vista, so whichever Windows operating system you're using now you should have the ability to encrypt your drives, provided you don't use older systems such as Windows XP (which Microsoft no longer supports and is considered insecure). Encryption is especially necessary if any of your staff have laptops. BitLocker encrypts Windows drives and protects from data leakage especially if the laptop is stolen.

If you have Windows 7 or a newer operating system, you can also use BitLocker to encrypt your USB drives. This is important if you share PHI or sensitive data using thumb drives between two computers.

Encryption is addressed in the Transmission Security standard (§164.312(e)(1)) as an addressable implementation, which requires the covered entity to determine whether it is reasonable and appropriate for their environment in accordance with §164.312(a)(1) of the Security Rule.

You should enable BitLocker on both your computers and your server. One requirement for BitLocker is a TPM (Trusted Platform Module). A TPM is a chip installed on the computer's, or server's, motherboard.

If you attempt to configure BitLocker on a disk drive that contains your operating system but don't have a TPM, you'll receive an error. You can override this requirement through security policies. Without a TPM, you will be prompted to enter a password before Windows is able to boot. This would be a good option for personal laptops. For servers and workstations, this may not be an ideal solution, as somebody would have to physically be present every time Windows is restarted (for example in the middle of the night when updates are applied).

Figure 8. On drives without TPM, Windows will prompt for the password before it can boot.

Note: Apple Mac computers include FileVault, which is similar to BitLocker, and can be enabled with just a few clicks.

Turn on BitLocker in Windows 2012

In this exercise you will learn to enable BitLocker to encrypt drives in the Windows server operating system. We will be using Windows Server 2012 for demonstration purposes. The example assumes that you have the required TPM hardware and it is properly enabled in the BIOS. Check with your server's manufacturer for detailed instructions.

 Note: BitLocker *is a very secure encryption method and as a result it is impossible to access your drives if you lose your recovery key. Before enabling BitLocker, make sure you fully understand what you are about to do or ask a professional IT specialist to help you.*

Install BitLocker Feature

1. Open **Server Manager**
2. Click Manage, then select **Add Roles and Features**
3. The "Add Roles and Features Wizard" opens. Click **Next**
4. Select "Role-based or feature-based installation" and click **Next**

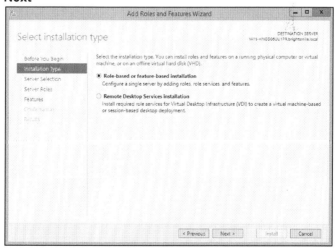

5. Click **Next** to confirm the default selected server
6. Click **Next** to skip Roles

7. Under Features, select "BitLocker Drive Encryption" and click **Next**
8. Click "**Add Features**" to confirm all required components
9. Click **Next**, and then **Install** to start the installation
10. The installation should only take a few minutes to complete and will prompt you to restart your server
11. **Restart your server**

Turn on BitLocker for the C: drive

1. Open **Control Panel**
2. Change view to **Large icons**
3. Select "**BitLocker Drive Encryption**"
4. Find the C: drive then click "**Turn on BitLocker**"

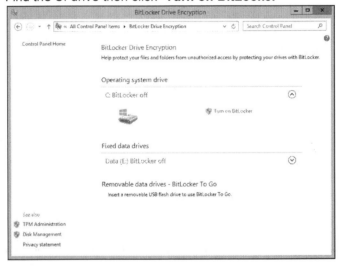

5. Windows will perform a brief check and search for your Trusted Platform Module (TPM). Resolve any errors at this point with your server's manufacturer
6. BitLocker will ask how you want to back up your recovery key. It is critical that you keep this in a safe place in case of emergencies
7. Click "**Print the recovery key.**" Take the printed document and store it in a safe place. I recommend you take it to your

home and store it in a safe location (possibly in a real safe!).

A recovery key will look like the example below and is uniquely created every time BitLocker encrypts a drive:

238530-525743-523480-479476-347651-604016-271158-041250

8. I don't recommend that you "Save to a file" because of the risk of the file being compromised. However, you can save it to a flash drive that you will be keeping safe and away from your place of business
9. Click **Next**
10. Select "**Encrypt used disk space only (faster and best for new PCs and drives)**" then click **Next**
11. Click **Continue**
12. Perform the same procedure for any additional fixed data drives, such as D:
13. **Restart your server**

Tip: Remember that you can encrypt both a hard drive and a USB drive. After you enable BitLocker, it will show in your system settings.

That's it. Encryption on your drives greatly reduces the chance that a third party can gain access to your data.

Summary

This chapter focused on getting you up to speed on client server architecture and the benefits of using a server. You should have a basic understanding of server hardware and how to make an informed purchase decision. BitLocker is a free encryption method to protect the data on your server's hard drive.

- ☐ **Identify your workgroup environment.** Determine if some or all of your computers are operating as a workgroup or are as part of a domain.

- ☐ **Identify your server.** Even if you do not have an actual server, find those computers and devices that are hosting applications and storing patient information.

- ☐ **Evaluate your server hardware.** Does your server have adequate resources, such as disk space and RAM? Does it provide data redundancy in case of drive failures?

- ☐ **Evaluate if any devices should be protected with encryption.** Any portable device with access to EPHI should be encrypted. Windows provides BitLocker, while Mac computers can use FileVault.

Up Next

Once you get your server architecture designed and set up, it's time to configure your network. Configuring a domain is much different than configuring a workgroup. I'll discuss domains and server setups in the next chapter.

Configure a Domain

Small offices rarely have a domain set up, but it's a more secure model than the standard workgroup setup. Domains take more work in the beginning to set up, but they also make managing your network security easier than in a scattered configuration of workgroup machines. In this chapter, we'll discuss domains and their advantages for better security.

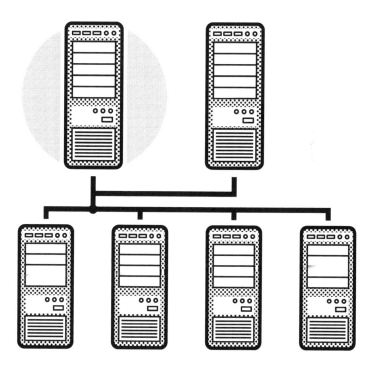

Figure 9. A Windows Server is used as the central point of management for all computers.

What is a Domain?

A domain is a type of client-server architecture. We discussed client-server architecture in the previous chapter. A domain is the software side of client-server architecture. It centralizes all kinds of network policies and security. For instance, if you want to control the version of software on all of your computers, you can use the domain controller to set up a policy for every computer in the network. You no longer need to go from machine to machine to identify software versions. You just create one policy from your server.

Domain Controller

The domain controller is a centralized server that controls these policies. It's the hub for all network settings and security. Because of its importance on the domain, this machine should never be a standard workstation used by any office staff. It should only be accessible by administrators. In a small office, you should have only one or two administrators, and they should understand the importance of domain controllers and configurations.

Computers in a Domain

Computers within the domain can still communicate with each other, and the domain controller "approves" the connection of a new computer. It also verifies a user's identity to ensure that they should be able to access local network resources. Since a computer joins a domain, a user can log in to any computer approved on the domain. If you have office staff that frequently move to different locations or between different offices, they can log in from anywhere connected to the domain and work. One note about these computers: You must upgrade your office computers to Windows Professional. You can do this for a small fee with Windows Anytime upgrade, so you can do it over the Internet directly inside the operating system.

Tip: You can upgrade Windows 7 Home Premium to the Professional edition by clicking the **Start** button. In the search box, type **anytime upgrade**, and then, in the list of results, click **Windows Anytime Upgrade**. If you have already upgraded Windows 7 to Windows 10, then you have to purchase a license for Windows 10 Professional either directly from Microsoft or from a software retailer.

The Power of Active Directory and Policies

At the center of your (Windows) domain is Active Directory, which is special software installed and configured on your domain controller – specifically a Windows Domain Controller. It's mainly a database for your domain, but it also gives you control over security properties, such as passwords.

Stolen passwords – whether from phishing or social engineering – are one of the most common ways hackers are able to access the internal network. For this reason, administrators should create password policies on the network. It's one reason Active Directory and a domain are beneficial for small office security.

Active Directory offers several options for password policies. The administrator can control the password complexity, length, and the amount of time needed before the user enters a new one. You can even block the use of repeated passwords in Active Directory.

I'm going to show you how to create policies and folder redirections, but first you should know that only an administrator should have access to these configurations. An administrator is the business owner or a trusted IT professional that can manage user permissions. You don't want random staff members having access to domain controllers. This leads to a security issue called "insider threats." Insider threats are one of the biggest cyber threats to an organization.

Getting Started with Active Directory

Active Directory is a role that a Windows server can use to manage users, groups, computers, policies, and more. Active Directory is quite complex and entire books are written to cover all the aspects of it. I'm going to show you the basics that you will need to get started.

Assign a Static IP Address to Your Server

In the following example, we are going to configure the server with a static IP address, which will be required later on when you are configuring additional network administrative features, such as DNS. An IP address is similar to a phone number assigned to your phone. Each computer or device on the network must have a unique IP address in order to communicate with one another. Typically, those IP addresses are handed out by a DHCP server, such as a cable modem or wireless router. IP addresses are made up of four sets of numbers, joined by periods. Examples of IP addresses are 10.0.1.11 or 192.168.1.199. The important thing to remember is that numbers can only range from 1 to 254 and on small networks only the last number is used to uniquely identify a computer. This effectively allows each network to contain 254 devices.

 Note: Setting an incorrect IP address will cause your server to be unable to communicate on the network and access the Internet. You can always reverse any changes by repeating the steps and selecting DHCP again.

Determine the current IP configuration

1. Go into the **Control Panel**
2. Change view to **Large icons**
3. Select "**Network and Sharing Center**"

4. Select your network connection and click on it. The default name is "**Ethernet**"

5. Click **Details** to show the current IP configuration
6. In the example below, we can see that the current IP address is provided by a DHCP server and the IPv4 is 10.211.55.30.

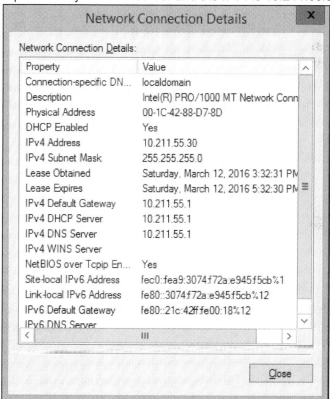

7. On a piece of paper, write down the following information, so we can reference it later:

IPv4 Address:
IPv4 Subnet Mask:

IPv4 Default Gateway:
IPv4 DNS Server:

Choosing a static IP address

This part can be a little tricky. Now that you have determined your dynamic address above, you need to determine a safe IP address that you can assign permanently to your server that is not going to conflict with the rest of your network. To do so, you will need to access the DHCP server to determine which IP addresses are safe to use. The DHCP server is typically your Internet provider's router (such as a cable modem or DSL modem), or a third party router such as Linksys or Netgear. Refer to the manufacturer's instruction about accessing and determining the DHCP settings. Most DHCP servers will use a scope (a range) of IP addresses, which are assigned to devices that connect to it. For example, a typical IP scope might start with 192.168.1.10 and end with 192.168.1.100. You will need to determine an IP address that is outside the current scope but still less than 254. For our example scope above, a good static IP address to use for our server would be 192.168.1.200.

Assigning a static IP to your server

1. Go into the **Control Panel**
2. Change view to **Large icons**
3. Select "**Network and Sharing Center**"
4. Select your network connection and click on it. The default name is "**Ethernet**"
5. Click **Properties**
6. Highlight "**Internet Protocol Version 4 (TCP/IPv4),**" then click **Properties**

7. In the "Internet Protocol Version 4 (TCP/IPv4) Properties" window, select "**Use the following IP address**"

8. Enter your newly determined static IP address from the previous step
9. Enter the Subnet mask and Default gateway you wrote down earlier
10. Enter the Preferred DNS server you wrote down earlier
11. Click **OK**
12. Click **OK** again
13. Finally, click **Close**

You have now configured a static IP address and if done successfully, you should be able to browse the web just like you did before.

Note: *If for any reason you were unsuccessful, you can repeat the last procedure and in step 7, select "Obtain an IP address automatically."*

Installing and Naming Your Domain

In this example we will be configuring our server to be the domain controller for your new domain. **Do not attempt to do this if you already have a domain on your network.** If you are already using a domain in your business, you will need to join your new server to your existing domain. The following example assumes that you do not already have a domain in place.

Add the required Active Directory role to your server

1. Open **Server Manager**
2. Click Manage, then "**Add Roles and Features**"
3. Click **Next** to skip the welcome screen
4. Select "Role-based or feature-based installation" and click **Next**
5. Accept the default server and click **Next**
6. Under Server Roles Select "**Active Directory Domain Services**"
7. Accept any required features and click "**Add Features**"
8. Select "**DNS Server**"
9. Accept any required features and click "**Add Features**"
10. If you are getting a warning that no static IP addresses were found on this computer, then cancel the setup wizard and assign your computer a static IP address like we did in the previous example
11. Click **Next**
12. No additional features are needed at this point. Click **Next**
13. Click **Next** on the "Active Directory Domain Services" overview
14. Click **Next** on the "DNS Server" overview

15. Click **Install**
16. Installation will take a few minutes to complete. When completed, **restart your server**

Set up your domain

1. Open **Server Manager**
2. Click the yellow warning symbol to reveal the notification window
3. Click "**Promote this server to a domain controller**"
4. Select "**Add a new forest**"
5. Give your domain a name including the extension **.local**. If you have your own website you could use the same domain, but replace the .com extension with .local. Other domain names typically reflect the name of the business. For our example, we are going to use 'brightsmile.local' *(Don't actually use this same domain name unless your business happens to be called "Bright Smile")*

6. Click **Next**
7. Leave all the default Domain Controller Options as they are
8. Type a secure password into the "Directory Services Restore Mode (DSRM) password" field.

   Make sure to use a strong and complex password, then

WRITE IT DOWN. Then store the password at a safe location away from your business. An example of a strong password is Xg4T#rsYa6

9. Confirm the same password
10. Click **Next**
11. Click **Next** on the DNS Options screen
12. Click **Next** on the Additional Options screen
13. Leave the default paths and click **Next**
14. Review the options summary and click **Next**
15. Click **Install** to start the installation
16. The server will restart automatically as part of the installation process

Protecting User Passwords is a Must

Although a user can log in from anywhere, users should never share their user name and password. HIPAA regulations require audits and logging on files and data. §164.312(A)(2)(I) requires that each user must be uniquely identifiable. If users share their credentials, you don't have accurate logs to fall back on should you need to review who accessed data. Always educate users to never share their credentials with anyone, especially someone who calls the office claiming to be someone from staff. This is a type of social engineering that I will discuss in future chapters.

The administrator can also override local policies on the computer. All aspects of the local workstations can be controlled from the domain controller, so you can keep each computer the same as others. This ensures that users have the right software and setup to seamlessly work together and also reduces compatibility issues.

How Active Directory Controls Passwords

Short, easy to guess passwords are an issue for HIPAA compliance. If you let users create simple passwords such as "12345," then you run the risk of these passwords being cracked. This is where Active Directory password policy options are beneficial.

 Tip: Password management is required and outlined in §164.308(a)(5)(ii)(D) and requires that passwords must be changed and safeguarded.

Password policies are found in the Group Policy Management Editor on a Windows Server. You can open this utility by typing "gpedit" in the Windows Run text box or by clicking the "Active Directory Users and Computers" from the main Administrative menu. I will cover Group Policy Management and policy for configuring a password in more detail in a later chapter.

The policy lets you configure many options, but the six you should pay the most attention to are shown here.

- Enforce password history: this option stops users from reusing the same password. In the image, the user can't use the same password for 24 password changes. You don't want users to have the same password for several changes, because it defeats the point of changing a password. 24 is a good standard, but you should at least set it to 10.
- Maximum password age: this option defines how long users can keep using the same password before they are forced to change it. Most companies force password changes at either 30 or 60 days.
- Minimum password age: this option stops users from changing their password multiple times to get by the password history filter. This setting can be left at 1.
- Minimum password length: this is the minimum length of the password the user can set. Passwords should be at least 6 characters, although most security professionals suggest 8-character passwords.
- Passwords must meet complexity requirements: this option requires users to use capital letters, special characters, numbers and letters. It stops cyber hackers from brute-force guessing the password. This should always be enabled.
- Store passwords using reversible encryption: this should always be disabled, because it allows the operating system to store passwords in encrypted form that can be reversed.

Summary

To summarize, we learned how to get started setting up Active Directory to make your network HIPAA compliant by improving security. Without a domain, you would need to manage and secure each PC, and you wouldn't have the same level of control for your programs or security that you have in a domain. Domains let you standardize a user's desktop and rapidly deploy new software, patches and updates to the operating system without managing the computers one by one.

- ☐ **Identify any domain controllers in your network.** Domain controllers are servers that use Active Directory to manage your domain. Multiple servers could have different domains, if they were configured incorrectly.

- ☐ **Identify all computers that can be joined to a domain.** Only Windows Professional computers can join a domain. Windows Home editions or portable devices, such as Microsoft Surface RT, cannot.

- ☐ **Upgrade Windows Home editions to Professional.** Microsoft's Windows Anytime Upgrade allows you to upgrade from Home to Premium in just a few steps.

- ☐ **Ensure each user has a unique login name.** Logins must be unique not just for Windows, but also for any applications, such as your Electronic Medical Records Software.

- ☐ **Identify passwords that do not meet security guidelines.** Look at all passwords, such as those used for logins, firewalls, electronic medicals, backups, wireless access, etc.

Up Next

Up next, I'll show you how to work with the Internet while keeping your internal network safe from malware.

3

The Internet Affects Your Security

The Internet is a necessity for most businesses. Even if you just have email, you need Internet access to send and receive messages. Unfortunately, Internet access for employees opens up a whole new world of possible vulnerabilities. Malware, keyloggers, phishing, and social engineering are just a few of the dark sides to the Internet. Even with these hazards, the Internet is a benefit to any organization. You can communicate with customers better, research information, and send data more quickly. This chapter will show you some of the safeguards you can use to protect patient data.

Time Wasters and Malicious Sites

There are two main websites you should block on the network: time wasters and malicious sites.

Figure 10. Some examples of common time wasters

Time Wasters Are Not Productive Resources

Time wasters are common social media websites. Facebook, Twitter, YouTube and Reddit are four common ones, but there are many others. According to a Salary.com survey, almost 30% of employees admit to wasting five hours a week or more at work on time-wasting sites. For this reason, organizations put access restrictions on websites accessible from work.

This should not be confused with efforts to market your business via social media. If you rely on traffic and referrals through social media, you need to allow for users to interact with visitors online. But ask yourself who that person should be. If you are the only one updating your organization's Facebook and Twitter feeds, then no one else needs that access and you can restrict all other employees from those sites. I'll say more about how to accomplish this later in this chapter.

Malicious Sites Are Out to Get You

The second category of websites to definitely block access to is malicious sites. These sites are more dangerous than time wasters, because they exist strictly to take advantage of naive users who don't know the warning signs. Hackers create numerous ways to trick employees into entering private information on phishing websites. They will create domains that are a few letters off from legitimate sites and make their website look like the popular branded domain. They then ask the employee to enter user names and passwords. If these user names and passwords are what can be used to log in to your network, then the hacker can gain access to your data.

This is exactly what happened in 2013 when Target lost millions of credit card numbers to attackers. The attackers were first able to penetrate the system using a phishing attack on Target's HVAC contractor. This led to the massive attack on their point-of-sale systems that allowed attackers to steal credit card numbers.

Who Let the (Malware) in?

Malware is also an issue with Internet access. Employees with unrestricted access can download software from anywhere regardless of the site's credibility. This software could be a virus, trojan, keylogger, or any other type of malware that gives the hacker access to the local machine. This type of access gives the attackers remote control of the machine, which means that they can perform almost any action on the network. This type of access is referred to as a "back door."

An example of this type of attack was the power outage in the Ukraine in 2015. Hackers were able to gain access to an internal computer by installing malware on it. This malware then gave the hackers remote access to the machinery. With remote access, they brought down power for 80,000 people in the Ukraine.

There is a distinct difference between each type of malware. I won't go through all of them, but here are the ones you should be concerned with.

- Viruses are small programs that don't usually self-replicate. They aren't as common with hackers, because they are mainly used to destroy data or crash a machine. Since the goal is to steal data, they aren't useful to hackers for anything other than mischief.
- A trojan is usually the starting point for hackers. These programs are installed on a machine silently and sometimes download additional software (brings it in with them, like the Trojan horse) which give hackers access to the machine.
- Ransomware is an especially nasty piece of malware. This malware encrypts data on a machine and holds it for a ransom. The ransom increases as the user waits to pay the ransom. In some cases, the user never gets the decryption key and loses all data. Backups are useful to protect from this malware.

Tip: You can use Group Policies to block certain URLs, but there are also several third-party vendors that offer content filters with predefined categories and a database of URLs. These third-party vendors make it easier to block entire categories of content, such as sites flagged as malware, porn, or malicious phishing sites. You can also use this software to track Internet activity and monitor suspicious traffic.

The Dangers of Social Engineering

Social engineering is on the rise. It doesn't take any technological know-how. Instead, hackers trick users into giving them information over the phone or through email. In some cases, the hacker convinces an employee to send personal details of other employees such as in the case of a recent social engineering attack on Snapchat. Even worse, social engineering is used to get employees to send money to the attacker's account.

The only real way to defend against social engineering is to educate your users. Always verify a user when they call. Hackers call employees with a variety of excuses and tricks to get the employee to give them credentials. They pretend to be an IT professional in need of credentials to fix a workstation, or an employee who forgot their login.

Some hackers use social engineering to get information on a particular user or patient. Sensitive patient information should never be given to someone without proper identification.

Phishing

The other way hackers get sensitive data is through phishing emails. Emails requesting data for what appear to be legitimate reasons. You can purchase third-party email filters to block suspicious emails. The emails are quarantined, so any false positives can be retrieved. However, most of the filters take care of phishing emails and spam used to trick employees into accessing malicious websites.

Your employees should be educated on the way hackers gather information about a target. Hackers read social media posts and profiles to gain insight on the employee, the business, the way the business operates and any pertinent information about personnel. Much of this information can be found on social media. Employees should know that they should never post private company information through social media channels.

Ways to Protect Yourself Against Internet Threats

1. **Always make sure your computers are up to date.** Software companies are constantly updating their code to fix security issues and improve usage. You should enable Windows Updates (or update your Mac) constantly. Below, I'll show you how to use a Group Policy to enforce Automatic Updates.
2. **Always use a good antivirus program.** As a Windows user, this may already be second nature to you, but it's important to stress it again. In addition, make sure that you are receiving notifications when a threat has been detected. Often, the user's input is needed to help the antivirus software clean a found threat. If you are not alerted, threats could remain on the computer for weeks.
3. **Train all users to employ common sense when using the Internet.** Explain to them that they should never just click on any popups asking them to install something.

Good software usually costs money and sites that offer free versions of popular software, such as Microsoft Office or Adobe Acrobat, usually are loaded with trojans or malware. If it sounds too good to be true, it usually is.
4. **Use web filtering tools to block access to known bad sites.** This is an easy solution that can prevent users from accessing the wrong sites in the first place. See later in this chapter for my favorites.

Enforcing Automatic Updates Across your Domain

1. Open **Control Panel**
2. Change view to show **Large icons**
3. Open **Administrative Tools**
4. Open **Group Policy Management**
5. Expand the forest, then the domain, then domain name until you see the Default Domain Policy
6. Right click on your domain name and select "**Create a GPO in this domain, and Link it here…**"

Create a GPO in this domain, and Link it here...
Link an Existing GPO...
Block Inheritance
Group Policy Modeling Wizard...
New Organizational Unit
Search...
Change Domain Controller...
Remove
Active Directory Users and Computers...
New Window from Here
Refresh
Properties
Help

7. Name the new policy "**Windows Update Policy**"
8. Right click the new policy and click **Edit**
9. Expand Computer Configuration, then expand Policies, then expand Administrative Tools, then expand Windows Components, and finally Windows Updates
10. Double click "**Configure Automatic Updates**" to open it
11. Select **Enabled**
12. Change "Configure automatic updating" to "**4 – Auto download and schedule the install**"
13. Leave the "Scheduled install day" as "**0 – Every day**"
14. You can leave the default time at 3 am, which I recommend you do if you leave your computers turned on at night. Otherwise set it to a convenient time throughout the day.

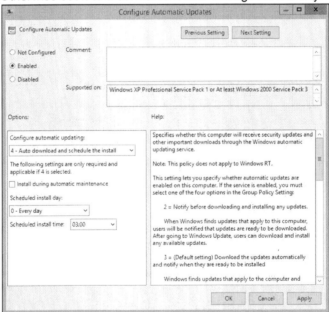

15. Click **OK**

Note: *Additional options let you fine tune the update process and you can read through each one to see what it does. I don't recommend that you make too many changes as it will be harder later on to troubleshoot if something doesn't work as expected.*

Good Free and Paid Antivirus Programs

Finding the right antivirus program is like finding the perfect pair of socks. After lots of trial and error you finally settle down on that perfectly comfy brand of socks, just to find yourself complaining about them six months later when they are worn out and full of holes.

Often times, it's the same thing with antivirus software. If you read yearly third party reviews, you often find that last year's number one is now in 6th place and the program that couldn't hold muster three years ago is now the new champ. Here are my favorites that have consistently performed well for me.

Examples of antivirus programs

Name	Comments
Webroot Endpoint Protection http://www.webroot.com/us/en/business	Easily the top contender. It's lightweight and offers good protection and is managed through a web portal.
Avast Business https://www.avast.com/en-us/avast-for-business	All managed through one online portal and basic antivirus is free. You pay for optional services, such as spam protection and firewall.
Kaspersky Small Office Security http://usa.kaspersky.com/business-security/small-office-security	Top scores for virus detection and removal in addition to Android protection.
MalwareBytes https://www.malwarebytes.org/business/	While not an antivirus app itself, it provides excellent protection and remediation against malware. Use in addition with other antivirus apps.

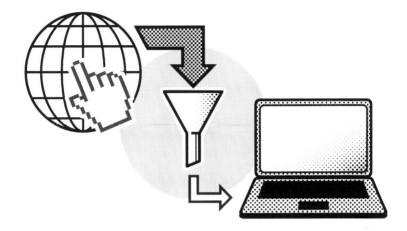

Clean your Traffic with a Good Web Filter

Preventing your users and computers from connecting to bad sites in the first place is a great way to minimize risk. But let me stress that this should not be used as an alternative to using a good antivirus software. They both serve different purposes and using one does not negate the other.

Domain names, such as Google.com, have to point to an IP address, which tells your computer where to access the site. When using a DNS based web filter, the service can trick your computer by redirecting bad site requests to safe pages. Let's say you went to ThisSiteWillGiveYouAVirus.com. Maybe you clicked on a link inside an email or you mistyped a website address (You might remember how for a number of years whitehouse.com was actually a pornographic website and not the symbol of leadership of our nation.). Instead of receiving the actual server's information, the DNS web filter would instead point you to an alternate, but safe page.

Software filters

Most DNS based web filters work the same way. You simply use their DNS servers instead of your Internet Service

Provider's. One advantage is that this change needs to be implemented only on your router or Windows DNS server, and then you're all set to browse the Internet safely. A drawback, however, is that DNS servers can be easily bypassed by savvy computer users by manually adjusting their computer's settings to use a different DNS server altogether. This can be mitigated by ensuring that users don't have administrative rights to make those changes. Also, viruses could potentially change your computer's settings or circumvent the filter altogether.

Recommended DNS based software web filters

Name	Comments
OpenDNS Umbrella https://opendns.com/enterprise-security/threat-enforcement/	Jam-packed with features that let you monitor and control any Internet activities
Dyn Internet Guide http://dyn.com/labs/dyn-internet-guide/	Free if you are using other Dyn services. Can correct typos such as gogle.com to google.com
Norton ConnectSafe https://dns.norton.com	Not as full of features as others, but offers simple protection from bad sites

Hardware filters

More sophisticated filters operate on a hardware level. The filter is embedded into a firewall or another stand-alone network appliance that has the capability of stripping network traffic at a much higher level and are therefore much more effective at halting attempts of trickery. Some stand-alone appliances, such as offerings from *Barracuda Networks*, are usually marketed for larger organization that can afford the high cost associated with the devices. We will talk about firewalls and their filtering options in a later chapter.

A more affordable hardware level filter comes in the use of certain firewalls. Many firewalls have the capability of adding filtering (usually as an option). I'll be covering firewalls in much greater detail in a later chapter.

Summary

In this chapter we reviewed the risks that are associated with the Internet, and how using filters, antivirus programs, and best practices can help reduce such risk.

- [ ] **Make sure updates are applied to all devices automatically.** Microsoft and other software providers continuously patch their software against security risks. You should always ensure your systems are up to date.

- [ ] **Use a good antivirus program on all devices.** Both Windows and Mac computers need to be protected against viruses. Make use of automatic alerts to be notified of any issues.

- [ ] **Train all users about Internet dangers.** Understand the threats of social engineering, phishing, and time wasters and set clear expectations.

- [ ] **Use web filters to block malicious and time wasting sites.** Whether you chose a software or a hardware filter, either can help eliminate bad sites and reclaim productivity.

Up Next

In the next chapter I will talk about one of the main benefits of having an Internet connected office, mainly the cloud.

4

The Cloud Brings More than Rain

You might not think you use the cloud, but the cloud is just another name for the Internet. Many of today's common services are moving to the cloud. These services are called Software-as-a-Service (SaaS). Any service hosted in the cloud is called a SaaS service. It's common for organizations to run several applications in the cloud instead of installing software on a local machine. This type of infrastructure has its benefits, but also has its pitfalls as well. For healthcare providers that need to stay HIPAA compliant, this new and widespread practice can be especially difficult to manage in light of the increased security requirements.

 Note: *Software-as-a-Service is the latest trend in computing, and in time, most software will contain at least some cloud component. Make sure you always read the fine print and ask the provider about their HIPAA compliance policies.*

If you decide to host any services in the cloud, you need to find the right provider. As a healthcare provider, the cloud service company must offer HIPAA compliant infrastructure and services. Email, for instance, is a cloud-hosted application. You don't want to use a non-secure email provider. Any connection you make to email servers must be encrypted, and use secure authentication. This goes for any other services you use to store EPHI.

Dealing with Cloud Providers

Before you search for a cloud provider, here are some basic questions you should ask as well as points for you to research.

- Are they US based? Non-US based providers aren't restricted by standard HIPAA regulations.
- Will they sign a Business Associate Agreement (BAA)?
- How do they secure their data?
- Are servers and services secured behind firewalls?
- What are their policies for data breaches and mitigation?
- Do they offer backups? How often do they back up your data?

Any SaaS application must be properly secured using HIPAA compliant security. Your service provider should be able to clearly explain how they secure your data. HIPAA compliant service providers usually have a separate type of service specifically designed for the increased security needs of healthcare providers.

Business Associate Agreements

A Business Associate Agreement (BAA) as specified in §164.308(b)(4) is an agreement between a healthcare provider and a HIPAA business associate (BA) (§164.308(b)(1)). Any BA that provides you with HIPAA-compliant systems and services is subject to periodic audits. Failure to comply costs the BA penalties and fees, and causes harm to their reputation.

At the start of your business relationship you need to contact the BA and ask them to sign one of these documents. If they refuse to sign, take your business elsewhere. There are plenty of others out there who will do things the right way. HIPAA compliant cloud storage providers (covered in the backup chapter) will sign a BAA with you. HIPAA-compliant host providers also sign BAAs.

It is also more and more common for cloud providers to include a BAA directly within their terms of service. In that case, they may not offer to sign your BAA but only because the protections are already provided to you. Instead, by agreeing to their terms of service, you are accepting their BAA.

For example, Microsoft's terms of service for Office 365 includes a BAA. Therefore, just by accepting their terms when you sign up for the service, Microsoft has provided you with a BAA.

 Link: *You can find for a downloadable Business Associate Agreement Template directly at http://www.spiffypresspublishing.com/hipaahealthy.*

Securing Email

Most offices have email, but they don't understand the importance of having secured email. With access to email, an electronic attacker can gain all kinds of information about the business and the employee and worse, your clients.

Email should always be sent over a secure channel. Free email providers are poor choices for healthcare providers. Companies such as Microsoft and Yahoo recycle unused emails. This makes your business vulnerable to attacks from users that register your old business name.

 Tip: Don't use free services from Yahoo, Google, or others for your business communication.

Another issue with free email is that electronic attackers are always targeting them with bots and scripted attacks. Your email addresses are then vulnerable and can be published on the web, and sometimes even the passwords are posted. Non-secure email makes no sense from a business perspective.

You should instead rely on hosted domain email that matches your secure domain. The provider you choose for SaaS and cloud services should also offer email service for your domain.

 Tip: If you already have a website with your own domain name, you can use that domain name with any email provider by forwarding email to it. Your domain name provider can make those changes for you.

Long Term Email Archival

HIPAA mandates that you keep a record of all emails for up to seven years if they contain EPHI. While you may not send patient information via conventional email (instead using encrypted email services or your EHR software), you don't want to find yourself in a situation where you should have kept a record, and didn't.

You can manually copy your emails to other folders, rely on computer backups, or pray that nothing will ever happen, all because you think the task of archiving is time consuming and difficult. The reality is that archiving email is a simple process that can happen seamlessly without your intervention.

 Note: Email archiving can be achieved by backing up emails with software or using a cloud service that intercepts and stores all messages that are sent or received by your organization.

Most email providers will offer this service as an add-on for just a few dollars a month. Once you enable it, you never have to worry about it again. Better yet, most services not only archive incoming emails, but also all emails sent by you or your staff. If your email provider does not offer this as an option, it may be time to find a better provider. At minimum, utilize a third party service to archive your messages for the long term.

 Tip: If you are using Microsoft Exchange as your email platform, you may be able to use 3rd party archival solutions by reconfiguring your mail flow.

Enterprise Level Email

You may think that you can't have the same level of email security and storage as large corporations, but you might be surprised to hear that a majority of small businesses have made the move to hosted Exchange. Exchange is a type of email service created by Microsoft. It has proven itself as a reliable service for many years now. In addition to email, Exchange mailboxes store contacts, calendars, tasks, and to-do lists. A major benefit of this type of email service is that all your emails stay synced with the cloud. In the unfortunate event that your computer's hard drive crashes, or your system fails, you will retrieve all your emails that are stored safely in the cloud. Google also offers a similar service called Google Apps.

Tip: *Microsoft Exchange and Google Apps also keep all your devices such as computers, tablets, and phones in sync.*

The best part is that you don't need to spend time and resources designing, building, and maintaining a system as complex as email. Many vendors offer hosted Exchange at very affordable rates.

Recommended Email Exchange Providers

Name	Comments
Microsoft Office 365 Business[3] http://www.office365.com	Enterprise level email with huge mailbox storage. Or upgrade your account to include fully licensed, up-to-date versions of Microsoft Office suite.
Intermedia Hosted Exchange[4] http://www.intermedia.net	US based, worry free email solution, with options such as email archiving, compliance, VoIP, and Backup.

Stop Spam Dead

Microsoft and Intermedia already offer top notch spam filtering capability. If your provider does not, you can make use of other services that function between the Internet and your web server. Spam filters are essential tools to eliminate viruses and malicious links from your emails. One company I've had much luck with personally is Reflexion. They offer spam filtering, email archiving, and email encryption services. More details can be found at http://www.reflexion.net.

---

[3] Microsoft's Online Services Terms include a Business Associate Agreement by default.
[4] Contact your Intermedia Sales Rep for assistance in obtaining a Business Associate Agreement.

Encrypted Mail

Whenever email is used to send EPHI, it is in your best interests not to use conventional email. Instead, look for services that offer encrypted email. Most EMR or EHR software will already have the capacity to send encrypted email messages. If not, look for hosted third party solutions. Some services have a completely web based interface that allows them to function just like Yahoo Mail or Gmail. Others offer plugins for Microsoft Outlook or other popular email clients so you never have to leave your favorite email program. In most cases, encrypted mail services are sold as a monthly subscription on a per-user basis for just a few dollars.

Examples of Encrypted Email Services

Name	Comments
Virtru https://www.virtru.com	Works with many popular platforms.
Reflexion http://www.reflexion.net/services/email-encryption/	No software to install. Encryption is triggered via configurable terms inside the email content.
Intermedia https://www.intermedia.net/products/encrypted-email	Plugin for Outlook or automatically scans messages.

Summary

The Internet is essential for business, but you must take the extra steps to ensure that your electronic connections to the outside world are secure from threats. Educate your staff about the dangers of social engineering and phishing attacks. With education, your staff is much less likely to fall into these traps. When searching for a cloud provider, always use a provider that is HIPAA compliant.

☐ **Identify any services that store data in the cloud.** Focus on software designed to store Electronic Health Records, such as cloud based EHR software, cloud backups, billing services, etc.

☐ **Get Business Associate Agreements for any vendor or cloud provider with access to EPHI.** Any vendor that has access to EPHI in unencrypted format must sign a BAA.

☐ **Ensure your email system is secure.** Older POP or IMAP accounts may operate over unsecured channels and can be intercepted by hackers.

☐ **Enable email archiving.** Use tools to keep copies of emails for long term record keeping.

☐ **Use encrypted mail for any patient sensitive emails.** Sending any EPHI must be done via encrypted email and is usually a separate process from traditional email.

Next Up

An essential part of protecting your network is using a firewall. I'll discuss how to use a firewall to protect your network from outside attacks.

5

Protecting Your Network with a Firewall

Firewalls separate a trusted network from an untrusted network (usually the Internet). Firewalls are required for HIPAA regulations, so you need one installed when you connect your office to the Internet. You don't need to know the technical details of a firewall, but you should know enough to purchase one and set up filters.

Why You Should Have a Firewall

I covered Internet threats in the previous chapters. The main purpose of a firewall is to protect from some of these threats. Another purpose is to separate your wireless connections from hardwired connections. A firewall sits between your Internet router and the internal network (illustrated below).

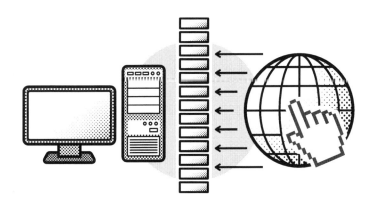

Figure 11. A firewall protects your computers from outside threats

There are several reasons that firewalls are required to make your network HIPAA compliant. First and foremost, firewalls are designed to block unauthorized access from the Internet to your data. This doesn't mean that simply having a firewall automatically secures everything.

Think of a firewall as an iron door bolted at all sides to the frame holding it in place. It's very secure and nothing will be able to penetrate it. But many organizations need to actually allow certain users access to internal resources. Maybe you work from home over the weekend, or your billing company needs VPN access to gather your patients' billing information. To facilitate this, the firewall needs to allow certain "ports" to be opened up. Think of it like tiny peepholes in your iron door. If not managed correctly, your iron door can soon look more like Swiss cheese than an impenetrable barrier.

Firewalls help by aiding this process and securing ports that should not be opened up. For small offices, firewalls can be pretty affordable with prices ranging between $300 to $500. Some optional add-ons and beefier specs can drive this price up to $1,000 or more.

 Note: Your Internet's router may already contain a simple firewall for basic protection, but true firewalls offer better protection and greater flexibility.

Recommended firewalls for offices with less than 10 computers

Name	Comments
Dell SonicWALL TZ300 http://www.sonicwall.com/products/tz300/	This entry level model is best for networks with under 10 devices. Optional content filtering and gateway Anti-Virus.
Ubiquity UniFi Security Gateway https://www.ubnt.com/unifi-switching-routing/usg/	Cloud based management and lots of add-ons, such as wireless access points, switches, VoIP.
Meraki MX64 http://meraki.cisco.com	Cloud managed dashboard with application visibility and control and content filtering.

Logging Firewall Events

One requirement that your firewall needs to perform is to log any activity and triggered events. This will later be used in case of a data breach and can help you track down what has happened. Some companies offer firewalls that are completely managed in the cloud through a web portal, which makes them very easy to maintain and makes keeping track of events simple.

Other firewalls require that you set up software (usually on your server) that will retrieve any events and store them long term. Such can be done with the popular software *Kiwi Syslog Server (http://www.kiwisyslog.com)*. There is a free edition, but I recommend the paid version for some of its extra capability. Not only can it receive events from computers (which I will cover in a later chapter), but it can also receive messages from firewalls, wireless access points, printers and more.

Note: In order to log events from your firewall you must configure its Syslog properties to direct all messages to the Kiwi Syslog Server. Use your firewall's manual with help on configuring it.

There are several firewalls on the market that log web events. As a matter of fact, it's rare to find a firewall that does not log events. To review a list of web events, log in to the Kiwi Syslog Web Access portal application and go to the Events page. This page gives you a list of events. You can filter events from this page, find specific events, and even export events to a CSV file. If you want to pause logging, you can pause logging from this screen.

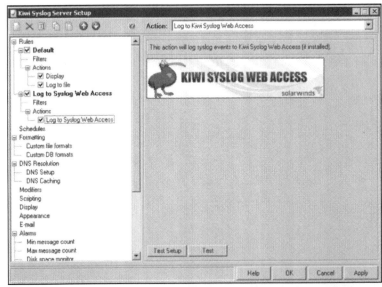

Figure 12. Kiwi Syslog server can store logs from various sources.

 Link: You can download Kiwi Syslog server from *http://www.kiwisyslog.com.*

Control Internet Traffic

Firewall software also provides you with filters to block certain content. Some filters provide you with a database of domains that you can block based on categories of topics. They also contain a list of sites that are flagged for hosting malware. These firewalls let you manually block content, send alerts to the administrator, or log activity on certain sites. All of these options help you during audits into suspicious network activity.

 Tip: Because the firewall is such a big piece of your security system, you should always set a strong administrator password. Not only does this protect from unauthorized access from external users, but it also protects from an employee making changes to the way you block and log Internet activity.

Figure 13. Communication over the Internet must always be encrypted.

Virtual Private Networks and Remote Access

Some offices provide remote access to the network. HIPAA has strong regulations for remote access. You must set up virtual private network (VPN) access, which means that the traffic passed from the user's remote location to the internal network "tunnels" within an encrypted, protected package. You must encrypt all traffic that passes through the Internet. This includes RDP[5] remote connections to the server or to another Windows desktop.

§164.312(a)(1) states that you are required to implement technical policies and procedures for electronic information systems that maintain EPHI to allow access only to those persons or software programs that have been granted access rights as specified in §164.308(a)(4).

Configuring a VPN is also something in the basic wheelhouse of a firewall. Follow the manufacturer's instruction on how to enable the VPN connection. Some firewalls use their own Windows or Mac based VPN client software, while others rely on native operating system configurations. Neither of them are that complicated to set up and should provide reliable and secured connections to your network across the Internet.

 Tip: Contact the manufacturer to help guide you with setting up a Virtual Private Network or hire a local IT professional to help you.

Prevent Personal Devices from Accessing your Network

In today's modern world, most people will have some sort of smart phone or tablet that they bring to work, and inevitably they are going to ask you for the wireless password.

---

[5] Remote Desktop Protocol (RDP) is a proprietary protocol developed by Microsoft, which provides a user with a graphic interface to connect to another computer over a network connection.

For HIPAA regulations, I highly recommend that you simply do not use or enable any wireless access to your network. Period. This will prevent unauthorized access and complex VLAN configurations on your firewall. If you can live without wireless, then this should be your best option. In addition, while some patients may want to use free Wi-Fi in your lobby, most will be understanding that you simply do not offer it to protect their valuable information.

If you do need wireless access or wish to use it, the next chapter will show you how to configure it in such a way to keep your network safe and still be in compliance with HIPAA regulations.

Summary

Firewalls are an added expense for your network, but HIPAA requires you to separate your wireless connections from the hardwired network. They also let you filter content and log web browsing, which will help with audits related to web access and activity.

- [ ] **Use a modern firewall.** Having a firewall is the first step in preventing intruders from accessing your network from the outside.

- [ ] **Identify any need for outside access into your network.** If you need remote access, make sure all traffic is encrypted or uses VPN.

- [ ] **Securely configure your firewall's settings.** Having a firewall is not enough. It must also be configured for maximum security.

- [ ] **Log firewall events for long term accessibility.** Depending on your device, third party software may be needed to capture and store firewall event messages.

Up Next

We discussed separating wireless connections from the internal network, so the next chapter will discuss setting up Wi-Fi, its advantages and disadvantages and the security behind Wi-Fi hotspots.

6

Protecting Your Wireless Network

Wireless access is great for mobile devices, but wireless networks present new vulnerabilities to your network. I discussed firewalls in the previous chapter, but I haven't covered Wi-Fi routers and security[6]. This chapter discusses the pros and cons of wireless connections and how it affects HIPAA security requirements.

Chances are good, in today's world of convenience, that you're going to ignore my recommendation from the last chapter and set up wireless Internet access in your office anyway. That's OK. There are ways to make your Wi-Fi secure so you don't have worry about unauthorized access.

Not every office needs a wireless router, but they have some advantages. If you have any medical devices that use the Internet, you connect these devices to a wireless router. Office staff can connect mobile devices to the wireless network, and you can connect wireless resources such as printers and tablets to the router.

---

[6] Most wireless networks are part of the internal network, which means any devices connected to it will not be secured through your firewall. It can leave your internal network exposed to outside threats if proper security measures are not in place.

Do's and Don'ts of Wi-Fi

- Do set a strong encryption password on your wireless network
- Do separate and isolate your wireless network from your cabled network
- Don't mix free patient guest access with your company network
- Don't give out the password to just anybody who asks
- Don't let employees use the company's wireless network for their personal devices (they should use the guest network instead)

Identifying Devices

One of the first things you do when setting up Wi-Fi is make a list of devices that need to use the service. Are there any printers or scanners in locations where a cabled connection is impossible? Do computers utilize wireless connections instead of wired connections? Do you own any new gadgets that use Wi-Fi to connect to the Internet, such as media players or music streamers, or Internet enabled devices such as thermostats, security cameras and alarms, or even doorbells?

Consider the Risks

After you have completed your list, you need to consider which of these devices actually need access to any EPHI system on your network or other data from your server. A printer or scanner likely needs to be on the same network as your computers in order to print to it. Tablets might be using software to connect to your medical records database to treat patients.

Devices that do not require access to data on your network, but simply rely on the Internet for their operation, should be handled in a different manner altogether. Those devices should never use the same wireless system that is connected to your cabled network. Keep them completely separated from the rest.

 ***Tip**: Identifying devices is part of the required Risk Analysis specified in §164.308(a)(1)(ii)(A) which I will discuss in a later chapter.*

Using Separated Protected and Open Wireless Networks

One easy way to keep your sensitive data away from risky devices is to have two completely separate wireless networks in place. The first is going to be attached to your existing wired network. Let's call this one the safe Wi-Fi. Devices attached to the safe Wi-Fi are allowed to interact with devices on your cabled network, such as your server, the same way that cabled computers are able to. They will receive IP addresses and configurations from the same DHCP server and utilize the same network settings as cabled devices. Devices connected to the safe network should only be allowed if they have a purpose that requires access to your secure network. The safe Wi-Fi should utilize the highest level of encryption available on your wireless router and use a very strong and complex password. Ideally, the password is not available to any staff and should never be handed out to anybody.

The second wireless network will be used for all other devices and can be made available for patients and guests. In order for this guest network to be completely separated, you are going to use your firewall. The configuration can get a little complex and technical, so you may need to employ the expertise of an IT guru or get help from the manufacturer. In essence, the wireless network will be placed "outside of your network." Some firewalls have built in wireless capabilities that let you configure secure guest networks with the push of a button. Other firewalls, or firewalls without wireless capabilities, can use several VLANs, which are virtual networks that can be configured not to pass any traffic between them.

Built-in vs Dedicated?

Some firewalls have built-in wireless capabilities, which makes them a very cost effective solution for a small office and work reasonably well if your physical office is not very large. In some instances, the location of the firewall is not ideally placed, which can cause the wireless signal to be extremely weak in some areas of the office. In that case, using a dedicated wireless access point that can be installed in a better, or more centralized, location is an option.

 Tip: Building materials can impact signal strength. As a good rule of thumb, try to have no more than two walls between your wireless access point and your devices.

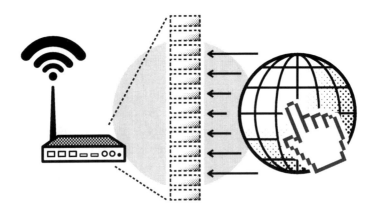

Firewalls with Wi-Fi Capability

For firewalls with built in wireless capabilities, configuration is typically a little bit more straightforward. Typically, you will be able to configure multiple wireless networks (such as a secure and guest network) using the same hardware. Each wireless network can then be configured to be a part of your wired network, or completely isolated from it. Many popular firewalls offer models with Wi-Fi capabilities for a slightly higher price. These are good options because no further hardware needs to be purchased or maintained.

Standalone Wi-Fi Access Points

When using stand-alone wireless access points, care must be taken to properly configure the firewall in such a manner to securely direct or isolate traffic from the wireless access point.

Recommended Wireless Access Points

Name	Comments
Ubiquiti UniFi AC https://www.ubnt.com/unifi/unifi-ac/	Affordable cloud managed wireless access points.
Meraki MR32 https://meraki.cisco.com/products/wireless/mr32	Cloud managed and high performing access point with complete visibility.
EnGenius http://engeniustech.com	Affordable access points with many model options, such as ceiling or wall mount.

Tip: Before making any purchase you should decide which wireless option is best for you. I recommend that small offices, where the firewall is centrally located, use a firewall with built-in wireless capabilities.

Configuring a Wireless Access Point

Every wireless access point has a security section. This section is where you configure the type of encryption you use. Most routers have the option for WEP and WPA, but WPA2 is the suggested form of encryption. WEP and WPA are still available to support older mobile devices that can't connect with newer encryption standards. However, every healthcare office should use the highest form of encryption, which currently is WPA2. When you configure the router for encryption, you will be prompted for a password. This is the password devices need to connect to the wireless network.

 Tip: Use WPA2 encryption and a very strong and complex password to secure your internal wireless networks. Keep the password in a safe place and do not share it with employees.

Hiding your Wireless from Snooping Eyes

Another security configuration you should make is hiding the SSID. The SSID is the "name" of your wireless network. When you go to a restaurant or coffee shop that has free Wi-Fi, you get the "name" of the Wi-Fi network to connect. This name is called the SSID, and you can configure yours in the access point's configuration application.

Most people change the name of the wireless network, add encryption, and give it a password and that's it. However, you can add a layer of security by hiding the SSID from broadcasting. Broadcasting the SSID allows an attacker to probe the network for any vulnerabilities.

In the SSID section, you can choose not to broadcast the SSID to hide it from the general public. You shouldn't allow the public to access your Wi-Fi network, so hiding your SSID from them isn't a problem. The one issue with this type of security is that you must remember the SSID and manually type it in to all wireless devices on your network.

Hiding the SSID is not foolproof. Any person with a little bit of experience can use software tools that detect hidden wireless networks. However, it's a good deterrent to keep the occasional snoop away.

 Tip: Configure a second wireless network that is completely isolated and separated from your internal network for all other devices, guests, and staff. Follow the manufacturer's instructions to complete this task.

Summary

Wireless connections provide your staff with a way to connect medical devices, smart devices, and remote workstations. It's also a gateway for hackers if you don't secure it properly. Remember from the previous chapter that wireless routers should be separated from the internal network using a firewall.

☐ **Identify any devices connected to your wireless network.** Use your access point's control panel to identify any connected devices, such as cellphones, tablets, computers, Internet enabled devices, etc.

☐ **Create a separate Wi-Fi network for guests.** Any devices that do not need access to EPHI should use a completely separate guest wireless network. Ensure that the guest network has no access to your internal network.

☐ **Use the strongest encryption method and Wi-Fi password.** WPA2 is currently the most secure method of protecting your Wi-Fi connection.

☐ **Hide your SSID.** Keeping your SSID from broadcasting does not make your Wi-Fi more secure, but it might stop visitors and patients from asking about it.

Up Next

Managing your data and knowing exactly where EPHI is located is extremely important. In the next chapter I'll talk about organizing folders and securing files and folders on your server.

7

Managing EPHI On Your Server

Keeping Everything Organized

Too often applications install files to default locations that are not necessarily easy to manage and organize later. Before adding any shared files, databases, or documents to your server, give some thought about the best way to administer them in the future. Having a well-structured file system makes administrative tasks, such as setting permissions, backing up, and monitoring much easier.

Security Management Process §164.308(a)(1)

You will need to identify all the EPHI within your organization. This includes EPHI that you create, receive, maintain or transmit. Check all of your computer workstations, laptops, tablets, etc. You might be surprised what you find stored on users' desktops, emails, and saved documents on the C drive.

- Make a written policy that states what documents should be saved, and where
- Redirect folders to your central server
- Train your users how to properly save documents

Note: Performing a risk analysis is required. You need to "conduct an accurate and thorough assessment of the potential risks and vulnerabilities to the confidentiality, integrity, and availability of EPHI."

Performing a Risk Assessment

A risk assessment is the process of determining potential security risks, and the probability of the occurrence and magnitude of such risks. In short, you want to find any weak points of your network so that they can be addressed. You can hire a specialist to perform a risk assessment for you (check your local community) or you can complete it yourself. I would only recommend you attempt to perform your own assessment if you have a firm grasp on security and a solid understanding of potential risks.

 Link: Find more information and links to the official Health and Human Services self-guided risk assessment tool at http://www.spiffypresspublishing.com/hipaahealthy.

If you would like to perform your own assessment, consider the following.

How does EPHI flow throughout the organization? This includes EPHI that is created, received, maintained or transmitted by the covered entity.

You must be able to answer the What, How, Where, and Who. What EPHI is accessed on each computer or tablet? Do all computers have the same programs and access to data? What sort of information is accessible on each device, such as images, billing information, patient records, etc.? How is the data accessed on each device? Is it accessible by using Windows Explorer and opening up a folder on the C drive or is it encrypted inside an application that requires secure user authentication? Is the data stored in encrypted format or could you easily copy it to another device to be accessed?

What are the less obvious sources of EPHI? Has the organization considered portable devices like PDAs?

Are you using special machines, for example X-Ray machines, that store data on local computers? Is this data left behind on the local computer after being transferred to the server? Are you using any mobile devices that store a copy of the data on its internal memory for faster performance? Can you access data on a portable device even when it's away from the office? This most likely means a local copy of the data is stored on the device itself.

What are external sources of EPHI? For example, do vendors or consultants create, receive, maintain or transmit EPHI?

You are using external sources if: you are outsourcing your patient billing process; you are using web-based EHR software; you are using cloud based backups for your files or databases.

What are human, natural, and environmental threats to information systems that contain EPHI?

Consider theft or malicious intent. If somebody stole your server, computer, or backup device, what access to EPHI would they have? How would a natural disaster affect your ability to access your EPHI? In the event of an Internet or power outage, what would you do?

 Tip: There are many potential risks to consider when completing your risk analysis and hiring a specialist will ensure nothing is missed.

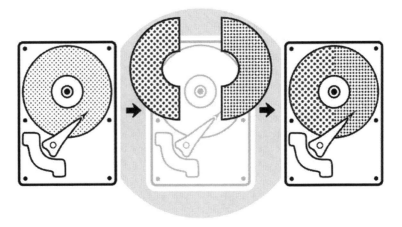

Using Partitions to Organize Data

Windows operating system files and program files reside on the C: drive. Odds are, when your server was built, the entire hard drive was using a single partition that spans the entire size of the drive. This is typically how personal computers are configured. For servers, I like to divide the hard drive into two partitions. One will be used for the operating system files and all program files, such as applications. The other is dedicated to storing actual data, such as your EHR's database, shared documents, patient records, and user folders. Typically, this partition is using the drive letter D. In Windows Explorer you would see a C and a D drive.

If your server is using a single partition, Windows makes it a snap to resize and create a second partition. When resizing the drive, a good rule of thumb is to allocate 1/3 of the total hard drive's size to the C drive, and the remaining 2/3 to the D drive. However, I recommend that your C drive not be smaller than 100GB.

 Note: Multiple partitions are not a requirement, but they help in organizing files on your server.

Creating Your New Partition

1. Go to the **Control Panel**
2. Switch icons to **Large icons**
3. Go to **Administrative Tools**
4. Open **Computer Management**
5. Go into **Disk Management**

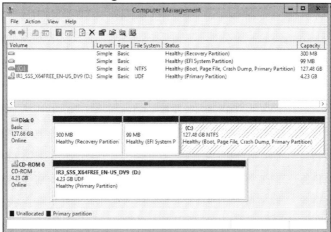

6. Select C: drive
7. Right click and select **Shrink Partition…**

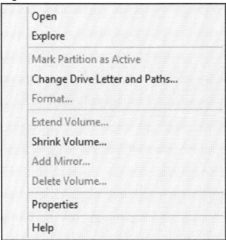

8. Take "**Total size before shrink in MB**" and multiple by 2/3. This will be the amount of space to shrink in MB. Round up to nearest number
9. Make sure that Total size after shrink in MB is greater than 100,000
10. Click **Shrink**
11. When complete, select new "Unallocated" space

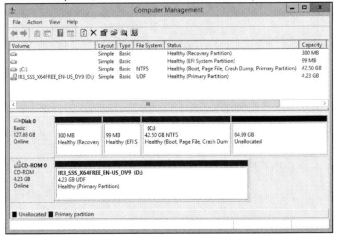

12. Right click and select "**New Simple Volume…**"

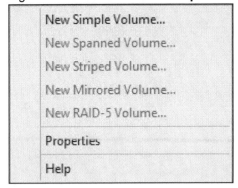

13. New wizard opens. Click **Next**
14. Leave the default simple volume size as is
15. Click **Next**

87

16. Make sure "**Assign the following drive letter**" is selected. By default, the wizard will choose the next available

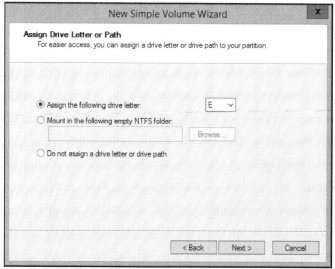

17. Click **Next**
18. Make sure "**Format this volume with the following settings**" is selected
19. Change "**Volume label**" to **Data**
20. Leave "**Perform a quick format**" as is
21. Do not check "**Enable file and folder compression**"

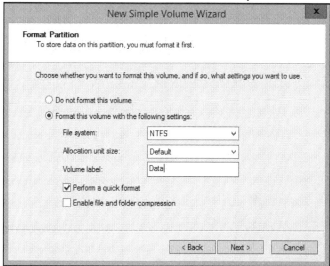

22. Click **Next**
23. Click **Finish** to complete the wizard
24. You now have a new drive in Windows Explorer

Redirect Folders to the Server

Your domain includes central servers for permissions and files. Therefore, files and folders should be redirected to a central location where you can back them up. Backups are necessary for HIPAA compliance, but they can be a nightmare if you don't have a central repository of storage. Users that store files on the local computer can lose those files if the drive becomes corrupted or you're forced to restore the machine from a recovery disk.

Luckily, a Windows domain lets you redirect any stored files to a central file server. I am going to show you how to set this up.

 Tip: *You can choose not to make files available offline in order to avoid making them accessible away from the office. This will prevent files from being accessed in case of hardware theft.*

Creating the Network Share

Before you start, create a directory on the domain server. This is where all of your user documents will be stored.

1. Open Windows Explorer and access your data drive
2. Right click and create a **New Folder**
3. Rename the new folder to **Users**
4. Right click Users and select **Properties**
5. Click on the **Security** tab
6. Click **Advanced**
7. Click **Disable Inheritance**, then click **Convert inherited permissions into explicit permissions on this object**
8. Adjust permissions to match the settings below

   > CREATOR OWNER - Full Control (Apply onto: Subfolders and Files Only)
   > System - Full Control (Apply onto: This Folder, Subfolders and Files)
   > Domain Admins - Full Control (Apply onto: This Folder, Subfolders and Files)
   > Everyone - Create Folder/Append Data (Apply onto: This Folder Only)
   > Everyone - List Folder/Read Data (Apply onto: This Folder Only)
   > Everyone - Read Attributes (Apply onto: This Folder Only)
   > Everyone - Traverse Folder/Execute File (Apply onto: This Folder Only)

9. Click **OK**
10. Select the **Sharing** tab
11. Click **Advanced Sharing...**
12. Select "**Share this folder**"
13. Leave the Share name as Users
14. Click **Permissions**
15. Highlight **Everyone** and click **Remove**
16. Click **Add...**
17. In the "**Enter the object names to select**" box type **Domain Users**, then click **OK**

18. Highlight Domain Users and place a check under **Allow** next to Full Control

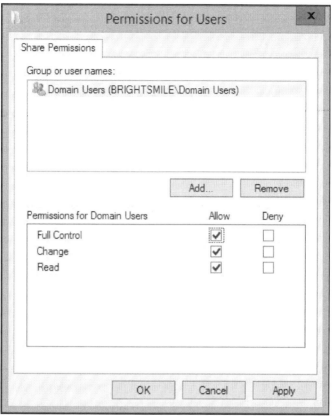

19. Click **OK**
20. Click **Caching**
21. Select "**No files or programs from the shared folder are available offline**"
22. Click **OK**, then **OK** again
23. Click **Close**

Using a Group Policy to Redirect User's Folders

1. Open Administrative Tools, then select Group Policy Management
2. Select your domain
3. Right click on your domain and select **Create a GPO in this domain, and Link it here...**
4. Name it **Folder Redirection Policy** and click **OK**
5. Right click on Folder Redirection Policy and select **Edit**
6. Expand **User Configuration**
7. Expand **Policies**
8. Expand **Windows Settings**
9. Expand **Folder Redirection**
10. Right click on Documents and select **Properties**
11. Under Setting, select "**Basic – Redirect everyone's folder to the same location**" from the drop down box
12. Under Target folder location, type the fully qualified UNC path of your User's folder share on the server. It should be **\\SERVERNAME\Users**, where SERVERNAME is the name of

your server.

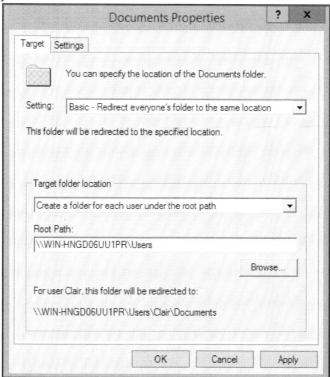

13. Select the **Settings** tab
14. **Uncheck** the box next to "**Grant the user exclusive rights to Documents**"
15. Check the box next to "**Also apply redirection policy to Windows 2000, Windows 2000 Server, Windows XP, and Windows 2003 operating system**"

 Note: You should not have any Windows 2000 or Windows XP devices on your network, as they are no longer HIPAA compliant. Microsoft has stopped support for those operating systems, and as such is no longer providing security updates and patches.

16. Click **OK**
17. Click **Yes** to acknowledge the warning
18. Repeat the same procedure for Desktop

19. Close Group Policy Management

The next time your user's workstation restarts, the new policy settings should take effect. When users log in again, all the files that are currently stored inside the user's local documents folder will be moved to the server.

Create a Folder for Shared Files

Now that you have configured the users' redirection folder, you can use the same method to create a shared folder for documents, files, etc. This would be a folder that is accessible by all users, or you can create multiple shared folders and adjust the sharing permissions for each by only allowing access by certain users or groups.

Summary

In this chapter I've shown you how to manage the hard drive space on your server and create a shared folder to store your users' documents.

- [ ] **Identify all EPHI inside your organization.** Check all computers and devices that create, receive, maintain or transmit EPHI. Don't forget about copiers and printers.

- [ ] **Perform a Risk Analysis to identify all weak points.** Determine the potential security risks and the probability of their occurrence as well as the magnitude of each risk.

- [ ] **Create a written policy that states what documents should be saved, and where.** All users must be made aware of where EPHI can be saved. For example, no EPHI should ever be saved to the local (unencrypted) workstation.

- [ ] **Organize files and folders on the server.** While having no effect on security, having properly defined file and folder structures will help make it easier to manage.

- [ ] **Redirect folders to the server.** Use group policy to define redirection policies for users' desktop and document folders.

Up Next

In the next chapter I will discuss users and groups in more detail and how to set access permission on files and folders.

8

User Accounts and File Level Security

Users and Groups, Oh My!

Keeping files secured is easily done with Windows Server. The first step is to assign a unique username for each user. §164.312(A)(2)(I) requires that you assign a unique name and/or number for identifying and tracking user identity. Luckily, Active Directory makes this process very easy.

User accounts

User accounts are unique names assigned to each user of your organization. Each person that accesses EPHI must have a unique username, this includes any staff at your local location, as well as anybody connecting to your server remotely, such as a billing company, via VPN[7].

Groups

Groups are organizational containers that can contain one or more users. Groups are often used to simplify managing rights and permissions, because they are easier to manage than multiple users. For example, a group called "*Billing*" could contain multiple users that should all have the same access to a billing related folder. The folder's security settings would then be configured to allow access for the *Billing* group, instead of having to enter multiple individual users. With proper planning, groups are essential to simplifying the security settings on a server.

---

[7] I previously covered Virtual Private Networks (VPN) in the firewall chapter.

Default Groups

Active Directory includes some default groups, such as Domain Users and Domain Admins. Refrain from making any changes to those default groups or you are at serious risk of breaking Active Directory or even locking yourself out from accessing or making any changes to it. Only modify users and groups that you have created yourself.

 Note: The Domain Users group is the default group that contains every user in Active Directory. It can be used for folders and files where every user should have the same level of access.

Creating a New User Account

1. Open **Control Panel**
2. Open **Administrative Tools**
3. Open **Active Directory Users and Computers**[8]
4. Right click on **Users** and select **New**, then **User**
5. Specify a "**First name**", such as John
6. Specify a "**Last name**", such as Smith
7. Notice how the "**Full name**" is automatically created

---

[8] This example assumes that your server is configured as an Active Directory domain controller

8. Enter a "**User logon name.**" I recommend using the first and last name, separated by a . (period). For example, john.smith

9. Type a secure and complex password, then confirm it again
10. Leave the default password options as is
11. Click **Next**
12. Click **Finish**

Creating a New Group

1. Open **Active Directory Users and Computers**
2. Right click **Users** and select **New**, then **Group**
3. In "**Group name**" enter the name of a group, such as "**Billing and Accounting**"
4. Leave the "Group scope" and "Group type" as is

Managing Members of a Group

1. Open **Active Directory Users and Computers**
2. Select **Users**
3. Double click on a group, for example Billing and Accounting

4. Select the **Members** tab
5. Click **Add...**
6. In the "**Enter the object names to select**" box type a username, for example john.smith

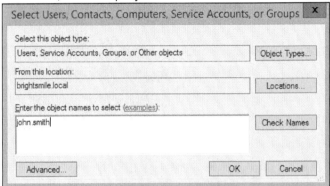

7. Click **OK**
8. Notice how John Smith is now a member of the group Billing and Accounting
9. Click **OK**

File and Folder Permissions

Now that you have created unique usernames and group, you can assign specific permission to shared folders[9]. Assigning permission to folders allows you to customize who is allowed to read or write documents inside folders. You can use security permissions to deny complete access, only allow read but not write, or allow full control over all files.

Sharing Permissions

Sharing permissions are similar to file and folder permissions, but instead of being applied to the file system layer, they control access to a share. You use sharing permissions to control access to files from a workstation. For

---

[9] If you are unsure about using security permissions seek the help of a local IT professional.

example, only users with appropriate permissions are able to open a file share. Users without the correct sharing permissions are denied access.

It is important to understand that you can allow a user access to a share, yet still deny access to particular files or folders. The table below should give you a basic understanding of how sharing and file permissions work in unison.

	File access is allowed	File access is denied
Share access is allowed	User has access	User does not have access
Share access is denied	User does not have access	User does not have access

Setting Access Permissions

At this point you might be asking yourself if you should set file and folder permissions or sharing permissions. Which one is the right one for you? Well, the answer is really a combination of both.

It is always best to define the users that DO need access, rather than the ones that do not. For example, let's assume we had a folder called "*Patient Billing Information*" that we wanted to share and make available only to members of the *Billing and Accounting Group*.

Creating the Folder

1. Open **Windows Explorer**
2. Select your data drive (for example, D)
3. Right click the empty white space and select **New**, then **Folder**
4. Name the folder "**Patient Billing Information**"
5. Right click Patient Billing Information and select **Properties**
6. Select **Security** Tab
7. Click **Edit…**
8. Click **Add…**
9. In the "Enter the object names to select" box type **Domain Users**
10. Click **OK**

11. Highlight Domain Users then place a check in the Allow column next to Full Control

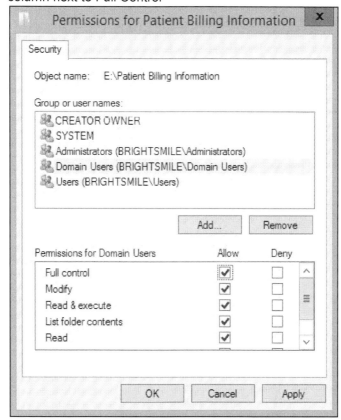

12. Leave the default groups as is
13. Click **OK**

 Tip: Always use groups when assigning permissions instead of individual users

By default, Windows uses certain security groups. Do not make changes or you risk getting locked out of the folder completely. Some groups are needed by the operating system to work correctly. For example, the SYSTEM account is used by Windows to access the files in order to back them up, run virus checks, etc. Without the SYSTEM account, Windows itself would effectively have no access to the files.

Sharing the "Patient Billing Information" Folder

1. Right click the "Patient Billing Information" folder and select **Properties**
2. Select the **Sharing** tab
3. Click **Advanced Sharing**
4. Check "**Share this folder**"
5. Click **Permissions**
6. Highlight **Everyone** and click **Remove**
7. Click **Add...**
8. In the "Enter the object names to select" box type **Billing and Accounting**
9. Click **Ok**

10. Highlight Billing and Accounting and place a check in the Allow column next to Full Control

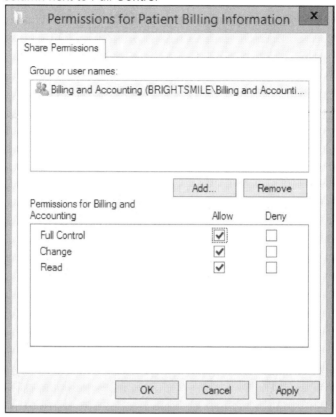

11. Click **OK**
12. Click **OK**
13. Click **Close**

 Tip: Never, ever use Everyone to set file or sharing permissions. The Everyone user is a special account that allows access from any computer, whether they are authenticated or not.

In the previous example, we have created a folder that allows all Domain Users full access. We then shared the folder and only allowed access for the Billing and Accounting group. The end result is that only users from the Billing and Accounting group are now able to access this share from their workstation. If you wanted to explicitly add one additional user who is not a member of the Billing and Accounting group, you could add that user to the share permission and allow access. Since file permissions are already set for Domain Users, the new user will be allowed access.

Summary

In this chapter we discussed various ways to control file and folder access on your server by using users and groups. Access to files and folders can be controlled by setting permissions on the file or folder level, as well as by setting permission on the share.

- **Organize users by groups**. Adding users to a group can help improve management when your organizations grows to more than a handful of users. Create groups by job responsibilities, such as billing, lab, accounting, human resources, etc.

- **Use group permissions for secure folders**. Very little information should be shared with all users. Secure all data according to job responsibilities.

Up Next

Backups are critical parts of HIPAA compliance and your business continuity. They are a part of disaster recovery plans, and they can save you days of lost work. In the next chapter, I'll discuss backups and the right steps to take to secure your data.

9

Backing Up Your Data

HIPAA requires that you back up data in case of a disaster. Disasters could be anything that puts you into a situation where you've lost critical information. It can be a natural disaster such as earthquakes or floods. It can be a fire. It can also be in the form of hackers gaining access to your system and destroying data. Backups are used to restore data, so you can recover from any of these disasters.

Figure 14. Backing up is the process of duplicating your data to another destination.

 Note: *Proper backups are required by §164.308(a)(7)(ii)(A) which states that you must establish and implement procedures to create and maintain retrievable exact copies of EPHI.*

Types of Backups

There are three main types of backups: full, incremental and differential. Whatever type you choose, you'll always need at least one full backup. You'll probably want to perform a full backup every once in a while, but you always start your backup process with at least one full backup.

Full Backup

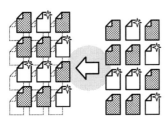

A full backup takes a snapshot of all your information. Most administrators limit full backups, because they take the most storage space, and they aren't necessary for every nightly backup.

Incremental Backup

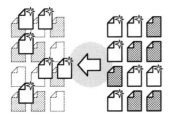

An incremental backup takes a copy of all files changed since the last backup. For instance, if you change two files since your last full backup on Monday, and on Tuesday you run an incremental backup, the process saves those two files. On Wednesday, four files changed since Tuesday's backup, so the next incremental will back up four files. After several incremental backups, you can then take a full backup and start the process again.

Differential Backup

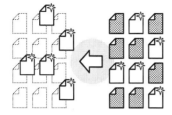

A differential backup is a bit different than an incremental. A differential backup requires a full backup. A differential backup saves all files that have changed since the full backup. For instance, you take a full backup on Sunday. On Monday, two files have changed and you run a differential backup. The differential saves those two files. On Tuesday, you run another differential and four files changed that day. A differential backup saves all six changed files, since you have a total of six that changed since the last full backup.

It's up to you which type of backup you choose as long as you have the storage space and correct process in place to back up your data each day.

The Modern Way: Image Snapshot

I mentioned three types of backups, but there is one more to consider. An image backup is a full snapshot of the entire hard drive. This means a full snapshot of programs, drivers, directory structure, and operating system. An image backup is a very convenient way to recover an entire machine or server. You don't need to reinstall programs or drivers with a full image backup. Just re-image the machine's hard drive, and you're ready to work again. These backups are convenient, but they take at least the same amount of space as what you've used on the hard drive, which could be several hundred gigabytes.

Tip: *I recommend that at minimum you take at least one daily full image backup to local disk and use offsite storage to backup documents, files, databases, etc.*

Recommended Backup Software

Name	Comments
StorageCraft http://www.storagecraft.com	Full backup and disaster recovery software with optional cloud storage for offsite backup.
Windows Server Backup http://www.microsoft.com	Free backup software included with Windows is best for daily full server backup to local disk, such as external hard drive[10]
Mozy https://mozy.com/hipaa	HIPAA compliant cloud backup with advanced features.
iDrive https://www.idrive.com/online-backup-healthcare/	HIPAA compliant cloud backup for basic files.

Choosing Storage for Your Backups

You can store backups on your local servers or you can use cloud storage. Both have their advantages and disadvantages. Any cloud service providers must sign a BAA with you, so you must find a cloud storage provider that is HIPAA compliant.

Keeping Things Local

You could keep the backups local, but this puts your backups at risk for disasters. If you store your backups locally and a fire destroys your servers, then you just lost your backups too. For this reason, many organizations prefer cloud storage as a way to host offsite backups. All you need is an Internet connection to retrieve these backups should you suffer from critical data loss.

---

[10] Windows Server Backup does not encrypt backups, so the storage destination must be encrypted using a tool such as BitLocker.

Off-Site Storage

In some cases, you can store backups on your local servers and schedule them to upload to the cloud. Just remember that large data transfers will eat away at your bandwidth, so you should perform these backups after hours. This type of backup process gives you a quick local copy should you need it, and then a cloud backup should you lose your primary local storage.

You also need to consider the local files you need to back up. You can use Windows Server Backup with BitLocker for local system files. StorageCraft is a cloud vendor that lets you back up your entire organization data to the cloud and encrypts it for security. Don't forget that you'll also need to back up any database servers. Most EHRs use databases such as MySQL or SQL Server. You need to back up these files as well.

 Tip: When backing up to a local drive, always encrypt your backups. You can use the backup program's encryption capability if provided, or use BitLocker to encrypt the entire drive.

Encrypting Your Backups

Backups are a main target for attackers, because they give a hacker complete access to all data and files. It can also give them access to passwords and other sensitive information to do more damage.

You need the right security to protect data. Encryption protects your data even if a hacker is able to gain access to the files. Encryption makes them completely unreadable by the attacker, but you will be able to decrypt the data with your own key. When you set up decryption, you're asked for a password. This is the decryption key you'll use to restore backups should you ever need them.

 Tip: Always use a very long encryption password. It is recommended that you use at least 24 characters, including random upper and lower case letters, numbers, and special characters.

The right cloud provider will encrypt your backups and help set up the synchronization between your local server and the cloud storage location. For instance, StorageCraft

ShadowControl can be configured to run on a dedicated backup server to protect against failure.

 Tip: Having a dedicated backup server makes recovery of EPHI much faster. In case of a server failure, the dedicated backup server can be used to access your EPHI temporarily.

I mention third-party software for backups and encryption, because this software gives you alerts and notifications should a regular backup fail, lets you schedule backups, and keeps your files organized. Using third-party software is much easier than manually managing your backups each week. It also lets you schedule the backups during off-peak hours, so your network performance isn't reduced during productivity.

Disaster Recovery Plan

A disaster recovery plan should also be in place should you need to use your backups during critical situations. A disaster recovery plan highlights all the steps you need to recover your data step-by-step. Instead of forgetting parts of your system or trying to remember recovery steps during stressful situations, a disaster recovery plan will remind you of what you need to completely recover your data.

 Link: *You can download a Contingency Plan Template directly from the HHS.gov website https://www.healthit.gov/safer/guide/sg003/*

Establishing a Contingency Plan

Having a backup in place is the first step to meet the requirements of §164.308(a)(7)(i). Next, write down the backup policy and the procedure for responding to an emergency or other occurrence (for example, fire, vandalism, system failure, and natural disasters). Just having a backup that you set-and-forget is not enough. All steps of the backup, as well as the restore process, must be documented[11]. In your contingency plan, answer the following questions:

- Do your procedures identify all sources of EPHI that must be backed up, such as patient accounting systems, electronic medical or health records, digital recordings or diagnostic images, electronic test results, or any other electronic documents created or used that contain EPHI?
- How do you start the process of restoring, or bringing back to operation, EPHI data?
- How does hardware affect your restore process? For example, if your server has a hardware issue that is causing it to be non-functional, how do you access EPHI?
- In case of catastrophic failure (such as the loss of the entire building) how do you plan on restoring EPHI data?

Emergency Access Procedures

One scenario you have to plan out ahead of time is how you would establish access to EPHI in an emergency situation. Depending on your practice's specialty, the term "emergency" may have different meanings, and it is up to you to establish a plan and safeguards to ensure that EPHI is accessible in case of an emergency. This plan should include the person(s) who will need access to EPHI in an emergency and describe, in detail, the procedures to make such access available.

---

[11] Plan on updating your Contingency Plan on a periodic basis to reflect changes in employees, procedures, data locations, etc.

Emergencies can come in many forms. Catastrophic losses could include disasters such as fire, earthquakes, or tornadoes that could completely destroy your place of business. However, much smaller issues are much more likely to occur and require more consideration. For example, a prolonged power outage would make computers inoperable; an Internet outage could make your web-based EHR software inaccessible; theft might result in loss of data or time spent purchasing and restoring data from a backup.

Tip: Make a list of applications that are critical in an emergency, then ask yourself how your practice would be able to operate without them.

Summary

Backups are the foundation for good disaster recovery. Even if you lose every hard drive in your server room, you can recover from cloud backup and recovery. To make it easier, you can consider third-party software that makes backing up your files an automated process. Just make sure you have the necessary storage requirements.

Having a contingency and disaster recovery plan is not just good practice, but it is also a requirement for HIPAA compliance. You must ensure that critical EPHI is available even in times of an emergency.

- ☐ **Identify local and off-site backup data.** Determine which backup procedures are currently in place and where they store your data.

- ☐ **Encrypt all backups.** Backups must never be stored in unencrypted form. Always use the highest level of encryption available to protect your backups.

- ☐ **Create a Contingency Plan.** Your disaster recovery plan needs to outline different scenarios and how EPHI will be recovered and brought back into operation for each. All steps of the backup, as well as the restore process, must be documented.

Up Next

You set up the perfect security, but you need to enforce it through group policies. The next chapter discusses how you lock down resources and enforce security policies for all staff members.

10

Enforcing Policies on Your Network

Enforcing security standards is a required part of HIPAA compliance. Risk management as addressed in §164.308(a)(1)(ii)(B) requires an organization to make decisions about how to address security risks and vulnerabilities. It is up to the leadership and management team to implement security measures sufficient to reduce risks and vulnerabilities to a reasonable and appropriate level to comply with §164.306(a).

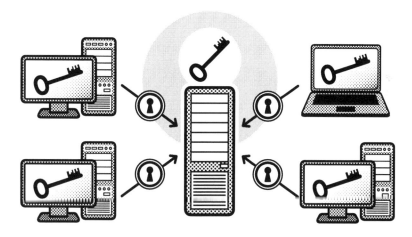

Figure 15. The central server is a key component in enforcing your policies.

Your network security is only as good as your enforcement policies. Windows servers have a utility called the Group Policy editor that allows an administrator to enforce the security rules across the entire domain. Each policy is called a Group Policy Object (GPO), so you'll see reference to "GPO" throughout the chapter. In this chapter, I'll show you how to work with the GPO editor, provide access rights for shared folders, and add biometric security to desktops.

 Tip: Many issues cannot be controlled by computer policies, but instead rely on people to adhere to them. Make sure all employees have a clear understanding of workplace rules.

Handling Policy Violations

Just establishing security policies is not enough if they are not being enforced. As stated in §164.308(a)(1)(ii)(C) you must apply appropriate sanctions against workforce members who fail to comply with the security policies and procedures of the covered entity. Using computer policies is a good step towards enforcing policies, but it is not enough by itself.

You can use group policy to force users to change passwords on a regular basis, but they cannot prevent users from sharing passwords with others or leaving post-it notes with their password next to their workstation.

You must address appropriate sanctions so that workforce members understand the consequences of failing to comply with security policies and procedures. It is not uncommon for violations to result in termination of employment.

 Tip: All sanctions must be written up and shared with all users on a regular basis. Don't treat them as something that "should just be understood" or as "common sense." You cannot expect all users to know all rules and regulations.

Enforcing Policies

The Group Policy Management tool is used to control various settings on your network to change how devices and users interact. All the settings are grouped by type to make it easy to control similar options. The image below shows you where to find the Security policies.

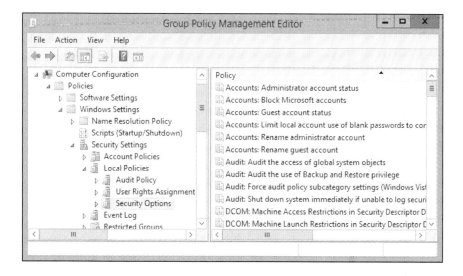

Notice that there are several options in this section. You need to go through each policy and determine if it's right for your organization.

Before you begin, you must be an administrator to edit GPO policies, and you need to log in to the server. Remember that very few people should have access to the administrator account, so either you or a trusted IT professional will need to make these changes.

Setting a Password Policy

1. Open **Group Policy Management**
2. Right click on **Default Domain Policy** and click **Edit...**
3. Expand **Computer Configuration**

4. Expand **Policies**
5. Expand **Windows Settings**
6. Expand **Security Settings**
7. Expand **Account Policies**
8. Select **Password Policy**
9. The default policy settings in Windows 2012 already provide good enough security, but you can change any value to meet your needs. Always leave complexity requirements enabled and reversible password encryption disabled.

Enforce password history	24 passwords remembered
Maximum password age	42 days
Minimum password age	1 days
Minimum password length	7 characters
Password must meet complexity requirements	Enabled
Store passwords using reversible encryption	Disabled

Disabling the Guest Account

Let's take a look at an example of one particular GPO—the "Disable the Guest Account" GPO. The guest account should always be disabled, because it's an unneeded account that stems from the older NT operating system when a "guest" might need to log in to the domain. It has no default password, which is terrible for security. Since all of your staff should have their own accounts, you don't need the guest account. For this reason, you can use the GPO editor to disable it across the network.

Scroll down to this option and double click it. You'll see a window similar to the image below.

1. Open **Group Policy Management**
2. Expand your **domain**
3. Right click on Default Domain Policy and click **Edit...**
4. Expand **Computer Configuration**
5. Expand **Policies**
6. Expand **Windows Settings**

7. Expand **Security Settings**
8. Expand **Local Policies**
9. Expand **Security Options**
10. Double click "**Accounts: Guest account status**"
11. Check "**Define this policy setting**" and select **Enabled**

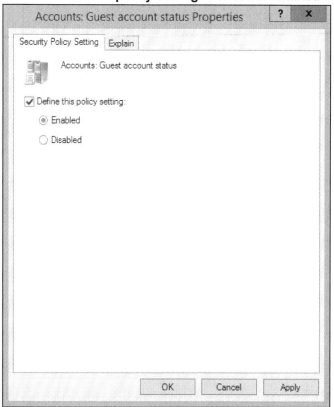

12. Click **OK**

Other Policies

You can enable and disable these policies by just skimming the list of security policies and enabling or disabling them. Before you change any security policies, you should also do a lookup on Microsoft's site to get a clear explanation of each security policy. Just one wrong change could be an issue for your domain's security.

Two security policies you should set are enforcing **screensavers with a password** and dealing with **logoffs** when users leave their computers for extended periods of time. Both of these policies follow HIPAA requirements.

Locking the Screensaver with a Password

A screensaver password policy locks the computer when a user walks away from the desktop and turns on the screensaver. You can also force the screensaver to show after a certain amount of inactivity time. This policy stops an attacker from accessing the network using the inactive user's credentials. Users should be trained to always lock their PCs (turn on the screensaver) when they walk away from the desktop.

1. Open **Group Policy Management**
2. Expand your **domain**
3. Right click on Default Domain Policy and click **Edit...**
4. Expand **User Configuration**
5. Expand **Policies**
6. Expand **Administrative Templates**
7. Expand **Control Panel**
8. Select **Personalization**
9. Double click "**Enable Screen Saver**" and select **Enabled**, then click **OK**
10. Double click "**Password protect the screen saver**" and select **Enabled**, then click **OK**
11. Double click "**Screen saver timeout**" and select **Enabled**
12. Change the "**Number of seconds to wait to enable the screen saver**" to **600** (10 minutes), then click **OK**
13. Expand **Computer Configuration**

14. Expand **Policies**
15. Expand **Windows Settings**
16. Expand **Security Settings**
17. Expand **Local Policies**
18. Select **Security Options**
19. Double click on "**Interactive logon: Machine inactivity limit**" and place a check next to "**Define this policy setting**"
20. Set the "**Machine will be locked after**" setting to **600** (10 minutes)

21. **Close** Group Policy Management
22. You can test the new settings by opening the command prompt on a workstation that is joined to the domain, and type "**gpupdate.**" (**gpupdate** is a command that applies any changes to the group policy to the local computer)

Tip: Remember you can set the screensaver timeout to any number of seconds. A good timeout limit is anywhere between 10 to 20 minutes.

Automatic Logoff

Automatic logoff is useful when users forget to log off of the network before they leave for the day (§164.312(a)(2)(iii)), however, there exists no such policy in Windows to perform this action. If your users don't log off the machine before leaving, it leaves your network vulnerable to attackers that have physical access to the office. This could even be another employee or even someone from the late-night cleaning crew. Always protect the network from virtual and physical attackers.

1. Create a written policy for all users and require them to log off the computer when they step away for longer periods of time or leave for the end of the day.
2. Enable the screensaver policy as mentioned above.

Stop Password Sharing

A note on password policies: you can enforce password policies, but you can't use GPOs to enforce password sharing. In small offices, it's common for users to share credentials to make access easier. Unfortunately, this goes against HIPAA compliance (§164.312(d)). Each time a user accesses a file or reads data, HIPAA compliance requires logged events. These events can later be analyzed if you've encountered a data breach. The only way to ensure that you have accurate logs is to require users to only use their own username and password to log in to the domain.

One way to protect from unauthorized users is to add a biometrics device such as a fingerprint reader on laptops and desktops. This ensures that the person logging into the machine is the identified user and not an unknown attacker with access to the machine.

 Note: *Violations for password sharing should be specifically addressed in your risk management policies.*

Use Biometric Devices to Avoid Typing Passwords

Biometric devices are a great way to quickly log into a computer. Technically, a biometric device is not replacing the use of passwords. Instead, a fingerprint can be associated to an account acting like a password. However, unlike typed passwords, fingerprints do not have to be changed frequently. You can find a wide selection of fingerprint readers on Amazon[12]. The "*Eikon Fingerprint Reader for Microsoft Windows Login and NEW Windows 10 Hello*" is a great choice if you are using Windows 10. No drivers are required to install it and it works with Windows 10 out of the box.

---

[12] Search your favorite online store for "USB fingerprint readers" to find one that matches your needs.

One caveat, your password policy is still going to force users to change their passwords on a periodic basis, and they will need to remember their previous password to update it. It's easy to forget the previous password, especially if you are relying on using a fingerprint, but don't ever fall into the temptation of writing down a password on a piece of sticky paper.

Written Policies and Training

It's not enough to have security on your domain through the server. Your users should also be aware of the common threats and have security policies highlighted. Most companies provide a security policy with employee manuals and training. This gives a clear breakdown of office IT security.

Security Awareness

Security awareness training has been shown to reduce cyber security risks for the organization. If just one phishing email gets through filters or an employee accesses a phishing site, it only takes this one time to suffer critical data loss. Ransomware and other nasty malware are commonly sent through email, so employees must be educated on the red flags when they open an email. For instance, they should know never to open a file attachment from an unknown source. If the attachment prompts the user to run macros, they should always decline and block the attachment from running unknown code.

Figure 16. Security awareness training has shown to reduce cyber security risks for the organization.

 Note: *Security awareness training can be done in-house or through an outside organization. It's a worthwhile investment to prevent from insider threats and social engineering.*

Social engineering is when an attacker is able to call a user and trick them into giving sensitive data. In some cases, social engineering has resulted in a user sending the attacker millions to an overseas bank account. This type of attack can be devastating for a small business.

Creating a Security Policy

When you create a security policy, list the top 10 best practices that can be handed to each employee. An example includes:

1. Never give your user name and password to a caller
2. Never give private healthcare information to a caller unless they verify their identity
3. Always lock your computer when you walk away from it
4. Always log out at night
5. Never share credentials with other employees
6. Change your password frequently
7. Use complex passwords that aren't easily guessed from personal information
8. Don't open email attachments from unknown senders
9. Never run macros from an email attachment
10. Never send sensitive data through email

Summary

Enforcing security policies helps educate your users and keeps the physical network safe from attackers. You can use several GPOs to protect your data, but user security awareness training will protect from attacks such as phishing and social engineering.

- [ ] **Use Group Policy to enforce passwords, disable the guest account, and enforce a screensaver time out period.**

- [ ] **Create written documentation to handle policy violations.** Your documentation should include rules to stop password sharing.

- [ ] **Use biometric devices.** Check with your software vendors if their applications support login with biometric devices.

- [ ] **Schedule recurrent training sessions.** Training should address security awareness and review all written documents and policy violations.

- [ ] **Create a written security policy.** Your security policy should be given to each user and updated often to address new risks. Post a copy in your organization's common area.

Up Next

Auditing and logging are both HIPAA requirements. You need to know who is accessing your data and when. The next chapter discusses auditing and logging access events.

11

Audit and Monitoring

In the previous chapters we have reviewed methods that can be used to prevent risk to EPHI. This chapter will deal with Information System Activity Review, a requirement as stated in §164.308(a)(1)(ii)(D). This required implementation is part of the Security Management Process standard. It states that covered entities must implement procedures to regularly review records of information system activity, such as audit logs, access reports, and security incident tacking reports.

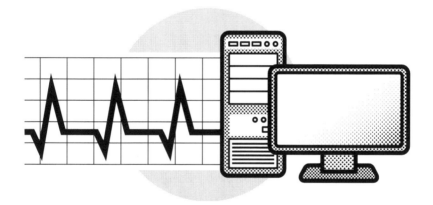

Figure 17. Auditing all activity is similar to measuring your computer's vital signs.

Definition of Logs

Logs are information that are recorded by an operating system or device about its functions, processes, etc.[13] A Windows event log can be configured to track file changes,

---

[13] The Windows Event Log contains thousands of entries about all aspects of the operating system. The challenge is identifying the log events that are actually needed for HIPAA compliance.

failed and successful login attempts, Windows errors, changes to Group Policy and Active Directory, and much more. It is important to note, that while Windows will log many events out of the box, some more verbose logging must be specifically configured in the local security policy. For example, while Windows will track failed login attempts (such as a wrong password used during a login attempt), it does not track successful logins by default. However, this can be enabled on all your Windows devices in the domain through Group Policy settings.

Logging and Reporting Requirements

HIPAA requires that you address the following for logging and reporting:
- Password Aging
- Consolidated Change Logs
- User Privileges
- NTFS Permissions
- System Privileges
- Role Permissions & Membership
- Remote Access
- User Access
- Auditing Enabled

This means that you will need to be able to produce reports that contain enough information to determine the date and time of a breach in EPHI, which system was affected, who initiated the breach, and in what manner EPHI was affected. Other reports include successful and unsuccessful logons and logoffs; successful and unsuccessful access to any security-relevant objects and directories, including creation, open, close, modification, and deleting; changes to Active Directory objects, such as user accounts, groups, passwords, and security permissions.

Collecting Logs

If this sounds daunting and overwhelming, it's because it is. Many of these logs require a lot of technical knowhow and the ability to tweak policies and settings to ensure the correct data is being logged. These tasks are often very complex. In addition, collection all of these logs creates a lot of generated data that must be sorted, filtered, analyzed, and reviewed.

I wish I could give you a simple suggestion or point to one software package that would take care of all of this for you. Wouldn't it be great if you could simply install one software and have it automatically configure all the policies, logs, filters, and reports for you?

Many software vendors would argue that their software can do these things or at least make the process easier. In my experience, however, I haven't found any software that lives up to that promise. That is not to say that there aren't several great software packages available to you that can perform some of the required tasks.

Note: *HIPAA requires that all audit logs be saved for 7 years. Make sure you use software that is capable of storing data for the long term and that you have adequate hard drive space available to store your logs.*

Employee Monitoring Tools

Many employee monitoring tools have evolved from spy tools or got their basic concept from spying software. They allow you to keep an eye on many activities your staff performs on their computer. Examples of activities you can spy, I mean monitor, are website activity such as the duration and frequency of visited websites, how long certain applications are being used, keylogging, automatic screenshots, file activity such as copy, delete and edit files, and more.

Ironically, while these sound like violations to employee privacy, most of these monitors are very useful for generating HIPAA required reports. These monitors give you full insight into any files that may have been copied to USB drives or uploaded to websites. All Outlook messages can be recorded to keep a record of patient communication. Lastly, employee monitoring tools can paint a comprehensive picture of what is happening in your environment.

However, there are some shortfalls with these type of tools. Primarily they have not been designed for use in a HIPAA-centric environment. That means reports are not always easy enough to read, and they lack abilities such as monitoring for changes to the Active Directory, or frequency of password changes.

Even with these shortcomings, they should be part of your arsenal in maintaining HIPAA compliance and make up part of your auditing strategy. If you feel like some monitors are in violation of personal privacy or that they are giving you reports that aren't required as part of your HIPAA auditing policy, you can always disable those monitors.

Examples of Employee Monitoring Tools

Name	Comments
Veriato 360 http://www.veriato.com/products/veriato-360	Monitoring and control tools needed to track and monitor all computer activity throughout your company.
OsMonitor http://www.os-monitor.com	OsMonitor can block most user activity, including website access, external drives and alerts when specific actions occur.
NetVizor http://www.spytech-web.com/netvizor.shtml	Monitor your entire network from one central location, including print jobs.
WorkTime http://www.worktime.com	60+ reports and tracks login/logout times, documents, computer usage.

Event Log Monitors

Event log monitors are basically log capturing applications that are designed to store massive amounts of logs and present them to you in the form of easy to read reports. Event log monitors do not actively audit anything on their own. Instead they passively ingest logs from other sources, such as Windows event logs, firewall logs, or printers.

Event log monitors are extremely useful as a single point of management for your entire infrastructure. The *WhatsUp Event Log Management Suite* from *Ipswitch, Inc* (https://www.ipswitch.com) allows you to generate reports about User Account Management, Object Access and Deletion, Password Reset Attempts, Computer Account Management and much more.

Examples of Event Log Monitors

Name	Comments
JiJi Identity Manager http://jijitechnologies.com	Free for under 500 users. Tracks changes to Active Directory, Group Policies, file servers and reports for HIPAA.
Netwrix Auditor http://www.netwrix.com/HIPAA_Compliance.html	Software designed for compliance audits with pre-built HIPAA reports.
Kiwi Syslog Server http://kiwisyslog.com	Passively collect & analyze logs, with real-time correlation, security analysis, and automatic responses
AlienVault USM https://www.alienvault.com/solutions/hipaa-compliance	Comprehensive reporting and log management for HIPAA compliance.

Figure 18. Event log monitors are used to store all events in a central location.

A big benefit of event log monitors is that they can include many detailed report templates out of the box but also allow you to create your own reports. Many event log monitors are designed for HIPAA requirements and will contain many of the reports that you will need to generate. They are primarily useful to generate reports related to Windows security, file access, and Active Directory.

A downfall of event log monitors is that they rely on software to generate logs. For example, Windows does not natively collect information about visited websites or application usage. Third party software is needed to generate that data. In addition, configuring Window event logs and firewalls can be challenging and also results in a lot of extra overhead on your server, if not done correctly. Even in a small network, I have seen hundreds of event log entries recorded every second. You will need to decide if that's too much information, or just enough!

 Tip: Look for log monitors that were directly written for HIPAA compliance or create pre-built reports for HIPAA. All the ones I recommended have this capability.

A Combination Approach

To cover all possible scenarios, I believe a combination of employee monitoring tools and event log monitors will lead you to the best result. Use employee monitoring tools on each desktop to record activities related to the usage of such device. Use it to record visited websites, local login events, changes to local applications, local file copies, etc. Then use event log monitor to collect Windows event logs and firewall logs, also known as syslogs, for long term storage. You can then use reports from both systems to generate compliancy reports.

Information System Activity Review

Now that you have set up logging and monitoring for all of your devices, you need to periodically review them. §164.308(a)(1)(ii)(D) requires that you implement procedures to regularly review records of information system activity, such as audit logs, access reports, and security incident tracking reports.

Tip: Use the built-in reports available in your monitoring and logging software to review any activity on a monthly basis.

Security Incident Procedures

You are required to implement policies and procedures to address security incidents. Defining security policies and procedures does not mean that security incidents won't still occur. Your organization is not safe from hackers, natural disasters, malicious intent, or just simple user error (accidentally emailing patient data to the wrong person or across unencrypted channels, for example). Even with a policy in place, protecting your business and yourself will take constant vigilance.

It is your responsibility to:
- **identify and respond to suspected or known security incidents** (*hacker, breach of data, etc.*)
- **mitigate, to the extent practicable, harmful effects of known security threats** (*implement policies and secure data communication, etc.*)
- **document security incidents and their outcomes** (*logs and monitors, etc.*)

There are too many possible incidents to list, but some examples are:
- **stolen or otherwise inappropriately obtained passwords that are used to access EPHI**
- Corrupted backup tapes that do not allow restoration of EPHI
- Virus attacks that interfere with the operation of information systems with EPHI
- Physical break-ins leading to the theft of media with EPHI
- Failure to terminate the account of a former employee that is then used by an unauthorized user to access information systems with EPHI

- Providing media with EPHI, such as a PC hard drive or laptop, to another user who is not authorized to access EPHI, prior to removing the EPHI stored on the media

 Tip: You should consult a lawyer who specializes in HIPAA to help you prepare security incident procedures before an incident occurs.

Summary

Auditing and logging are both HIPAA requirements. You need to know who is accessing your data and when. In this chapter I gave you examples of software that can help you log events and monitor your data.

- [ ] **Review and understand logging requirements.** Determine which computers and servers have events that need to be monitored.

- [ ] **Install an employee monitoring tool.** Any workstation that has access to EPHI needs to be monitored. Keep in mind you only need to monitor items that will help you prevent breaches or allow you to see what has happened when something goes wrong.

- [ ] **Set up a HIPAA compliant log monitor.** Configure software to collect event logs from any devices that store EPHI and automate reports and notifications. Don't forget to also collect firewall events to track any attempted breaches.

- [ ] **Schedule monthly reviews.** Set aside time to manually review collected logs to spot any unauthorized access to EPHI.

- [ ] **Create security incident procedures.** Define security policies and procedures to address security incidents. You should try to cover all possible incidents, but don't worry if you miss a few. You can tweak this document continuously in the future.

Up Next

In the next chapter I will discuss ways to protect your data from physical threats, such as theft or acts of nature.

12

Physical and Environmental Safeguards

Security policies and passwords are the primary way to protect your network, but physical security is just as important as virtual security. Monitoring is also a necessity. Unfortunately, insider threats are the biggest risk to the organization. In this chapter, we'll discuss how to physically protect the network, monitor your office, and use encryption where necessary.

Physical Security

Even in a small office, physical security is necessary and a part of HIPAA compliance. You must be able to physically secure your computers from insider threats. For instance, a cleaning crew could steal data that isn't physically secure. Some social engineering hackers have been known to enter buildings to gain access to data using USB drives or other removable media. Physical security and monitoring prevents this type of attack

Figure 19. Don't overlook low-tech security risks.

The first physical prevention is an alarm system. This is usually an easy one since the office should already has an alarm system installed. It can't prevent an intruder, but it's a reactionary measure to scare away thieves should they attempt to break into your office and steal equipment.

Servers should always have physical security. Servers should be behind locked doors. In bigger companies, the doors are equipped with ID swipe badges to provide an audit trail of anyone who enters the server closet. Server cages are also an option. These cages cover all sides of the servers to prevent access to the servers without a key or swipe card, should someone enter the server closet.

Server Rack Cabinet Enclosures

A server rack (some people refer to it as server cage) is a cabinet designed to securely hold servers and other networking equipment, such as network switches, firewalls, and network cable patch panels. Some racks only consist of rack posts and are open on all sides. You typically find open racks in locked server closets. Security racks have lockable panels on each side, so that the equipment inside cannot be accessed.

An example of a quality server cage is a Dell NetShelter SX Rack Enclosure (http://www.dell.com/us/business/p/rack-enclosures/pd) and pricing starts around $1,000. You can use it to install rack mountable servers, but they can also accommodate shelves for standard tower servers.
For the most part, any networking equipment should be behind a lock and key. Most offices use one room as a server room, but remember that the room needs plenty of ventilation and should be cooled continuously. Server rooms heat up very quickly, and this heat (if it isn't dissipated) can damage computer equipment. For small offices that typically only have one server, make sure there is plenty of air circulation to vent the hot air away from the server.

Tip: Train your staff to not stack boxes and paperwork on top of or next to the server. Allow at least 4 feet of space around the server.

If you have any backup devices in a separate location, they must be secure as well. If you use cloud backups, your data is backed up to a data center, which should have high-end security equipment. If you sign a BAA[14] with a provider, then you know that the proper physical security is applied to your rented equipment.

Tip: A low cost method for physically securing a server or backup device is to use Computer Security Cables that are anchored to a physical structure.

---

[14] I previously addressed the Business Associate Agreement (BAA) in the Cloud chapter.

Lock Your Backup Devices

Onsite backups need to be protected as well. Remember that backups have all of your data, so they are the most valuable to attackers.

- Keep your backups behind a locked door, and always provide good security for them.
- Only administrators should have access to your backup files.
- I covered off-site backups, but just a reminder – any onsite backups are vulnerable to fires and natural disasters. You should have an off-site backup in case of theft or natural disasters.
- An optional way to protect onsite backups is a fireproof safe. These safes can protect your media from both intruders and natural disasters.

Chain of Trust

Part of security and data recovery is a chain of trust among your employees. The administrator is usually the business owner or a trusted IT professional, but you also need a chain of trust should you need to have office staff access critical data. Remember that you should never give the administrator user name and password to other employees. Employees can be given temporary access passwords. This still follows auditing and logging rules, and you can still monitor any suspicious user behavior.

A chain of trust is used during emergency situations when the administrator isn't available. Trusted employees could have the ability to physically access the server should an IT professional need to work on the machines or give access to the premises when the administrator is away. The employees in such a chain should have good security training to understand social engineering and phishing scams so they can identify the red flags.

USB Flash Drives and Removable Media

Finally, one of the biggest mistakes that administrators make is the use of unsecured USB flash drives. These drives are small devices that can fit into a pocket and plug into a machine's USB port. It's easy for employees to steal data without anyone seeing it. You can disable USB devices through GPO policies, or you can physically disable them in a computer's BIOS settings, or by the use of USB locks.

Note: If you choose to disable USB ports through the BIOS, always password protect access to the BIOS settings to avoid unauthorized users from making changes.

Tip: Many employee monitoring software can be configured to block access to USB drives or monitor their usage.

Workstation Usage Policies and Procedures

One place not to overlook security is in your physical workspace. You have to ensure that your monitor is not in plain sight of anybody not authorized to view it. Just positioning your desk or angling the monitor away might be enough to stop glances. If that is not possible, consider using a screen privacy filter. You can find privacy filters at virtually any office supply store or online from places such as Amazon. They come in many sizes and can be cut to size if required. A filter works by creating an invisible area when the screen is viewed from any angle except straight on.

Create a written policy for all of your employees that documents physical attributes of the surroundings or a specific workstation or class of workstations that can access EPHI. This policy includes many items I've previously discussed, such as password policies, locking the computer when leaving the workspace, using screensavers, etc.

Tip: At minimum, all safeguards required for office workstations must also be applied to workstations located off site, such as employees working from home or in remote locations.

Encrypting Data

HIPAA requires that you encrypt sensitive data such as social security numbers and medical information. This includes any data transfers, stored lab results, and any data stored through your office applications.

Data transfers happen any time you move data from one location to another. It's especially necessary when you transfer data over the Internet. Never transfer data through unencrypted communication. You leave your patients' information exposed to vulnerabilities, and it's a clear violation of HIPAA requirements.

I've already briefly covered tools such as BitLocker that will encrypt data stored on your hard drives. For data stored in a database, always research the software available to ensure you find one that encrypts data in the database. Some application vendors advertise their product as HIPAA compliant, so you know that the data is encrypted on the backend. This is especially important if you have a public-facing website that gathers data. This data must be encrypted in case an attacker is able to access the data stored on the web server.

Handling Devices and Removable Media

Sooner or later, drives will fail. Whether it's a server, a workstation, a backup drive, or a removable device, it's inevitable to experience failure at some point. But just because a drive has failed (maybe it won't boot the operating system) does not mean that all data on it is now inaccessible and you can just throw it in the garbage without a care. Often times, only parts of a drive will fail, which is enough to cause the operating system to fail to boot or access data in any reliable way. However, with the right tools, remaining parts of the drive can still be accessed and recovered.

It is important that you treat any drive as if it has actual EPHI on it. Therefore, you must destroy the device to be 100% certain that no more data can be retrieved from it. Do not bring it to your local recycling center, as they are not governed by HIPAA security rules. Instead look for a local HIPAA compliant recycling or shredding service. Many paper shredding service companies also provide secure, HIPAA compliant device disposal for a nominal fee.

Tip: I have seen people use an electric drill in order to destroy a drive by drilling a few holes. This can be an acceptable method as long as you can assure the drive is beyond repair.

Re-Using Media and Devices

In cases where devices are being re-used, such as re-deployment in a new computer inside the organization, or externally, such as donating old computers to a local charity or school, it is important to remove all EPHI previously stored on the media to prevent unauthorized access to the information.

It is important that you do not simply delete items and leave them in the computer's "trash." Even emptying your trash does not permanently remove data. Many tools are available that allow deleted data to be restored. Instead, use a "**secure eraser**" tool, such as one included with many popular antivirus program (*Webroot's Secure Erase* or *Kaspersky's File Shredder*).

Link: An even better solution is to securely wipe the entire disk by using data wiping software such as DBAN (http://www.dban.org).

Continued Training

When you put these security measures in place, educate your employees to ensure that they understand why they are being enforced. When employees understand the risk, they are more likely to follow security policies. With security awareness, they are also more likely to see red flags to avoid social engineering.

 Tip: *Schedule quarterly reminders to review written documents and policies regarding security and workstation usage.*

Summary

Physical security is just as important as policies on the network. Always make an effort to keep critical equipment such as servers, routers, switches, backup servers, and database servers behind a locked door. Preferably, you should have ID swipe badges to keep track of anyone who accesses the server room.

Finally, always encrypt your data. Any data stored on a public-facing server such as a web server must be encrypted. HIPAA requirements call for encryption of data stored on web servers or any database that can be accessed from the Internet.

- [ ] **Install an alarm system.**

- [ ] **Secure physical access to the server.** Put the server in a locked room (with adequate ventilation) or secure it in a locked server rack.

- [ ] **Lock backup devices in a safe or with cable locks.**

- [ ] **Create a chain of trust.** Make sure everybody in the chain of trust understand their role and responsibility in an emergency situation.

- [ ] **Define workstation usage policies and procedures.** Any monitors in view of anybody not authorized to view it, such as the reception counter, must be angled away from view or protected with a privacy shield. The same goes for any other areas where unauthorized views might occur.

- [ ] **Implement training on acceptable workstation usage.** All users must understand the policies and correct work area usage.

☐ **Use encryption for all removable devices.** Any device that is used to transport EPHI, such as a flash drive, must be encrypted.

☐ **Destroy all data before disposing of any device or computer.** Make sure that no traces of EPHI are left behind before disposing of any old equipment, drives, tapes, etc.

13

Final Summary

By now, you should have a complete understanding of how you want to structure your network security – both physically and in terms of domain controllers. I'm going to highlight some of the basic points we've covered.

1. You Need a Good Server
You have to break out of the workgroup environment and centralize security and control of your network. This can only be done with a client-server environment. Servers are much more powerful machines, so they cost more than a regular workstation. However, you must invest in a good server machine rather than use a standard workstation. For a fully functional and efficient client-server environment, you need a powerful workhorse with plenty of resources to handle your user traffic.

2. Set Up a Domain
A domain is a networking environment that provides you with the tools and the software to control network security in your office. It provides you with ways you can enforce your security policy and ensure that user machines are automatically locked and logged off. It limits user activity on the network, and you can even centralize all file storage and backup procedures. A domain is required for centralized security, so you must invest in setting up a domain and eliminating the workgroup environment on your network.

3. Secure Any Internet Enabled Devices
The Internet is the primary weak space for your internal data. Any Internet access points should be monitored and filtered. You might need third party software to properly monitor and filter Internet access. Third party software

provides a database of known malicious sites that you can filter from access. Don't forget email as well – you need to filter malicious email that contains attachments or phishing links. Any wireless access points should be separated from your main internal network with a firewall.

4. You Need a Firewall
If you're using a workgroup environment, you probably don't have a firewall installed. You need to install a firewall to be HIPAA compliant, especially if you have a wireless access point. The firewall separates the external Internet from your internal network. It also lets you filter traffic, monitor access, and some firewalls send alerts when they detect suspicious traffic. There are several firewalls on the market, but all of them do an effective job of protecting you from unauthorized access to your network.

5. Protect Your Wireless Access Points
Most offices provide wireless access points for employees and mobile devices. Never provide wireless access for customers, especially on a wireless access point shared by your employees. All wireless access points should use encryption – specifically, they should use the WPA2 encryption standard because others have been cracked. For added protection, you can hide the SSID, so casual browsers can't find your wireless network ID. The wireless access point must be completely separated from any hardwired routers or connections.

6. Always Have a Backup Procedure
Backups are another HIPAA requirement. Backups are critical parts of a disaster recovery plan. They contain all of the information you need to recover from a disaster including physical disasters such as fire or virtual disasters such as a successful hacker attack. Backups will have your office back up and running within a few hours instead of suffering from data loss. Backups can be kept local, but you must have a remote backup in case the internal server room suffers from a natural disaster.

7. Enforce Security Policies

Enforcing policies is a two-step procedure. You first need to create a written policy to help employees understand the do's and don'ts for security. These policies also help your employees understand why you have security policies in place. The second step is to enforce security policies through your domain controller through Active Directory. Active Directory and Group Policy Editor work together to ensure that your security policies are enforced across every computer on your domain.

8. Audit and Log All EPHI Access

Use audit and logging tools to keep track of any access to EPHI. All users should be given their own unique user accounts to log into computers. Logging tools are used to record any time EPHI is read, modified, or deleted. Monitoring tools are useful to track users' behavior on their computers. Periodically audit all your logs and run HIPAA specific reports to review what is happening on your network.

9. Physical Security

Physical security is as important as your virtual security policies. Physical security includes alarm systems, locks and keys for the server, and security cameras to monitor the premises. You need physical security to protect from outside threats that use social engineering to gain access to the physical machine. With monitoring and physical security, you can ensure that no one can access the machine at the workstation.

Whether you or an IT professional configures your network, you must have HIPAA compliance implemented as a healthcare provider. These security measures not only safeguard your patients' information, but they also protect you from expensive fines should you have a HIPAA audit on your security policies.

Index

A

Active Directory · 25, 97
Alarm System · 148
Antivirus · 45
Audit · 135
Automatic Logoff · 126
Automatic Updates · 43

B

Backup · 107
Backup storage · 111
Biometric · 128
BitLocker · 17
Business Associate Agreement · 53

C

Chain of Trust · 150
Cloud · 51
Cloud Provider · 52
Contingency Plan · 116
CPU · 10

D

DHCP · 26
Disaster Recovery Plan · 115
DNS · 47
Domain · 23
Domain Controller · 24

E

Electronic Protected Health Information · 1
Email · 51, 54
Email Archival · 54
Emergency Access Procedures · 116
Employee Monitoring Tool · 139
Encrypted Email · 58
Encryption · 18, 152
EPHI · *See* Electronic Protected Health Information
Event Log Monitor · 141
Exchange · 56

F

File and Folder Permissions · 100
File system · 81
FileVault · 18
Filtering · *See* Web filter
Firewall · 61
Firewall Events · 63
Folder · 81
Folder Redirection · 89

G

Google Apps · 56
GPO · *See* Group Policy
Group Policy · 119
Group Policy Management Editor · 33
Groups · 97
Guest · 122

H

Hacker · 38
HIPAA · 1

I

Icons · 4
Information System Activity Review · 135, 143
Insider Threats · 25
IP Address · 26

K

Keylogger · 39

L

Log · 135
Logging · *See* Log

M

Malware · 37, 39
Memory · 11
Monitoring · 135

N

Network Share · 90

P

Partition · 84
Password · 33
Password Policy · 121
Password Sharing · 126

Peer-to-peer Network · 7
Phishing · 41
Physical Security · 147
Policy Violations · 120

R

RAID · 11, 12
RAM · 11
Ransomware · *See* Virus
Redundant Array of Independent Disks · *See* RAID
Removable Media · 151, 152
Report · 135
Reporting · *See* Report
Risk Assessment · 82
Risk management · 119

S

SAS · 12
Screensaver · 124
Security · 97
Security Awareness · 130
security groups · 103
Security Incident Procedures · 144
Security Management Process · 81
Security Policy · 132
Server · 8
Server Rack · 148
Sharing Permissions · 100
Snapshot · 110
Social Engineering · 40
Software-as-a-Service · 51
Spam · 57
SSID · 78
Static IP Address · 26
Storage · 11

T

Time Wasters · 38
Training · 154

Trojan · 39, *See* Virus
Trusted Platform Module (TPM) · 18

Virus · 40
VPN · 66

U

USB Flash Drives · 151
User Accounts · 97

V

Virtual Private Network · *See* VPN

W

Web Filter · 47
WEP · 78
Wireless · 69
Workgroup · 7
WPA2 · 78

Made in the USA
Middletown, DE
11 July 2025

10484423R00102